Journey in Inspiration

A Theological Novel

Richard P. Belcher

"Thy Word is settled in heaven, forever, O Lord."
Psalm 119:89

ISBN 1-883265-14-2

Richbarry Press

105 River Wood Drive, Fort Mill, SC 29715

Printed in the United States of America

Contents

AUTHOR'S PREFACE

We continue to marvel at the wide acceptance of our "Journey" novels---*A Journey in Grace, A Journey in Purity, A Journey in Authority, and A Journey in the Spirit.* During the interval between the publication of the next book in the series, people constantly ask when the next book will be ready, and what will be the subject area. Thank you for your encouragement as we seek to continue the series.

We reiterate that these books are not autobiographical in any strict sense, that is, the exact experience of the writer. Some of the events have happened in his life, but not all of them. However, most of the events have taken place in some ministerial setting, as it has been the author's privilege to know and counsel and fellowship with and encourage preachers and student pastors for many years. We have found the truth is indeed stranger than fiction.

Also it will be helpful to any reader to know that our desire is to help and encourage the church of our day in a very practical and understandable manner. It has been our burden for years to bring the truths of theology down to the level of the common man, and to present those truths in an interesting and gripping manner. Scholars have their place, and we thank God for their labors, but the people of God in the local church need someone to champion their cause, and to seek to inform them of the theological issues of the day.

To that end this book and the previous "Journey" books, and any future books in this series is dedicated. The people of God for too many years have been blown around by every wind of false and weak doctrine. True revival of His church, and the true building of the church is dependent not on the schemes and inventions of man, but upon the truth of the Word of God, the subject of this book.

1

Whose Voice Is This...?

I never imagined that I would go three years without a doctrinal challenge, especially since I had been pulled previously by divine providence into four pursuits in a matter of a few years.[1]   Perhaps it had been the impacting sorrow of the last one, which had brought so many mixed emotions in the process, including the betrayal and death of one I thought was a friend.[2]   Or perhaps it had been the push to finish college in the midst of pastoring Unity Baptist Church on the edge of the city of Collegetown.

And again in the summer of 1976, it didn't look like I would face another doctrinal pursuit, as I was planning to head off to seminary. I would have to drive 150 miles one way twice a week, while I still lived in Collegetown and pastored the church. That certainly would take all my time. The Lord had provided a fellow pastor to share the ride with each week, which would help pass the time of travel, plus save some wear and tear on my car, as well as myself, as we would also share the driving duties.

My traveling companion was Herby Hoskins, a vibrant young pastor, who had a burden for the lost, such as I had never seen. The story was that Herby would witness to anything that breathed, and then sometimes he would even corner objects that did not have life nor breath. He was a joy to be around, as he always wanted to talk about Jesus, the Word of God, or the need to reach a lost world for Christ.

When the day arrived in September, we made our way in the morning over the 150 miles, thankful that most of the route was interstate. We were a little bit apprehensive, like kids headed to the first grade, because we didn't really know what to expect. There were rumors and stories that the denominational seminary we were going to attend was somewhat liberal, with questionable doctrinal positions which veered from the orthodox faith. We knew it would be a venture of faith in many ways, both in our ability to do the work, and in the uncertainties of what we might face in the way of challenges to the truth.

We had already gone up a few days earlier to pre-register, so this was the first day of classes. We had a class in Bible survey in the early afternoon, and one in the area of Systematic Theology in the evening after supper. We would eat lunch every day at school, then take the classes. But at our first lunch experience there, something happened, which shocked the life out of me.

Herby and I were sitting at the table in the dining area with several other students, just getting acquainted, when a shocking familiar voice I thought I would never hear again reached my ears. Not only was it the voice that shook me, but the vocabulary and style of speech. The speaker was behind me, so my first contact was just by sound. It was the voice of someone greeting a student.

"My dearly beloved Brother Simpson! Did you enjoy your summer, even with its vanishing loveliness as tender as the flush of the rose leaf and as ethereal as the light of a solitary star?"

The words? The voice? The inflection? The exuberance? It was the voice and speech of Durwood Girvin!!! Or perhaps I should say, James Seavers!!![3] But how could it be!!?? He was dead!!! He had been dead, so I thought, for three years now!!!

As I spun around to catch a sight of the speaker, I almost fainted!! There standing at the next table was none other than Durwood Girvin!!!!! I thought I was staring at a ghost, and I was surprised that Girvin or whoever it was, didn't have a look of surprise when he saw me as our eyes met. Soon, though, his eyes focused back on the one he was addressing, and he hadn't even seemed to notice me. My mind went back to the way he had deceived me, the way he had misled so many people by his false doctrine and actions, and the way he had died in utter sorrow as he continued to embrace the lies of the enemy.

I left the table, made my way over to him, and waited behind him until he had finished his conversation. As I listened carefully through that exchange, I was convinced it could be no other than Durwood Girvin! When he turned to leave, I stopped him, and trying not to appear too surprised, nor to be a threat to him, I was about to address him, and without mincing any words.

---

[1]See the three previous "Journey" books by the same author and published by Richbarry Press (Columbia, SC): *A Journey in Grace* (1990), *A Journey in Purity* (1996), *A Journey in Authority* (1996), and *A Journey in the Spirit* (1997).

[2]See *A Journey in the Spirit* (1997).

[3]Ibid.

Who Are You...?

When our eyes met again, as I was trying to speak, I expected a look of shock to cross his face, but there was not even a ruffle in his expression, or a break in his bold and confident demeanor.

"What can I do for you, my dear young student of the greatest learning institution of this nation?" he said with a smile. "Come, come, young man! Spit out that slow thought that is creeping like a cold worm through your brain!" He spoke with great arrogance, especially since my words were slow in coming.

"Are...are...are...you...uh...Durwood Girvin?" I finally was able to ask.

"Durwood Girvin? Oh, you mean James Seavers! I surely would hope not! He joined the dismal march of death and has been diverted into alien channels like our dreams that fade and die in the mist. Or could it be that I am he, and he was me, as we both were caught in the cruel exchange of destiny as well as identity."

I couldn't believe it! He spoke like Girvin, and even seemed to enjoy the same cruel word games Girvin had played.

"Well, if you are not Girvin, who are you?" I asked, not knowing if I would get a believable or understandable answer.

"I, kind friend, am Samuel Seavers, the identical twin of James Seavers, alias Durwood Girvin! I have the blessed privilege of shocking students and then pouring knowledge into their empty brains as they attend my classes. And who are you sir? How did you know James Seavers?"

I explained to him that I pastored in the same city as had his brother, and we had become friends. I asked him if he had attended the funeral, and if so, why I had not seen him. Surely a twin would have stuck out in the crowd.

"Oh, I was in Europe enduring with a smiling composure the endless pursuit of a doctorate, and I could not come to the funeral. Were you the chap, who flushed from the minds of the people the fleeting touch, but intrusive hand of death which had stalked and taken my brother?"

I suppose he was asking if I had handled the funeral service and I answered in the affirmative. As I tried to read him, I already had heard a few statements that raised questions about his theology. I only hoped I could get through this school without having to take his classes. If he spoke that confusingly in class, who could possibly understand him?

"Well, Mr.,...uh...what's your name?"

I answered, "Ira Pointer."

"Well, then Mr. Pointer, let me thank you for preaching my brother's funeral, and for being a friend to him. He was really a strange follow!" he said, using normal speech now. "Anyone who made friends with him, or should I say, anyone who he let make friends with him, must be a special person, for he had major problems. But, I suppose I am not telling you something you do not already know."

Then he switched back into his exalted speech.

"Well, my good brother, I have a class--which will open the opportunity for the feeding of scholarly curiosity, but which will also call upon me to endure with smiling composure the presence of people who are at times distasteful in their actions as their dreams and visions of their simple theologies are challenged and destroyed. I hope to see you in one of my classes soon, Mr....uh, what did you say your name was? Oh, yes, Mr. Pointer."

And with that, much in the same style of his brother, he was gone.

Herby had stood by during the discussion with his mouth wide open?

"What was that all about?" he asked, full of confusion. He had not come to our area until after the Durwood Girvin event.

"I'll tell you on the way home!" I said, as we grabbed our briefcases and made our way to our first class. It went well, but little did we realize the surprise that awaited us in our class after supper that evening!

Which View Is the Most Ridiculous...?

As we entered the room for our Systematic Theology class that evening, it was buzzing with activity, being the first meeting of the class, but there was no sign of the professor. I asked Herby what the teacher's name was, but he didn't know. His class listing was in his brief case, as was mine.

And then the professor entered! It was none other than Samuel Seavers! I opened my brief case as he pulled his notes out, and I checked the class roster, and sure enough, it indicated that Samuel Seavers was the professor of our class. I hadn't even paid any attention when registering, because I had not expected any such possibility.

I noticed that we opened the class without prayer, certainly not an absolute necessity, but perhaps an indication of our direction. Then our teacher began to speak.

For a few moments he introduced himself, and then launched into the first area of our study---the nature of the Bible. He set before us a question about the Bible's inspiration, and he did it in a very graphic, even offensive manner.

He informed us that he was going to give us several views that people held about the Bible. One of them, he said was the most ridiculous and impossible of them all. He asked us to identify which one fit that category. Then he stepped into action.

First, he took a Bible and began tearing pages out of it and throwing them to the class. He said there is one view of the Bible which does that very thing. That view declares that the Bible is full of errors, and it cuts therefore from its contents many pages and portions of pages, leaving very little as authoritative for us.

I thought some of the men in the class were going to come unglued, and to be honest, I was ready to. Herby couldn't contain himself. Without being recognized, he spoke out.

"Sir, I resent what you are doing. The Bible is the divinely inspired Word of God, and you are blaspheming God in ripping it apart! I find that very offensive!"

The room lit up with a chorus of "Amens," and I thought someone was going to bolt to the podium and stop him.

With a continued arrogance and boldness he answered them.

"Oh, are you men fearful of having your cherished beliefs challenged? How do you think you will ever face an unbelieving world, if you cannot control yourself in a theology class? Maybe you're afraid of analyzing your beliefs."

He stood and gazed at them, almost daring them to leave or challenge him further. No one did, so he continued.

He put an overhead up which read as follows, even commenting on each view::

Which View Is the Most Ridiculous?

1. The Liberal or Modernist view which leaves little or no truth in the Bible?

2. The Neo-orthodox view which says that the Bible is the fallible human witness of the revelational encounters that the authors had with God?

3. The Errancy view which sees the Bible with some truth and some error? He said various people divide the truth and error in different ways:

   a. Some say the revelational parts are true while the non-revelational parts are not

   b. Others say the gospel parts are true while the non-gospel parts are not

4. The Dynamic view which says that God gave to the authors the thoughts, but they chose the words, which means the wording could and does have errors, but the truth still comes through without error?

5. The Dictation theory which says that God wrote the Bible through men and that he so overpowered them and blocked them out that the result is a Bible in its originals which is infallible and inerrant to its very wording?

He opened the floor for discussion, and most of the men in the class said the first one, the Liberal view, was the most ridiculous and damaging to the Word of God and its truth! I sat listening, trying to figure out where he was taking us.

Finally he spoke, and declared that the most ridiculous and horrible view of inspiration was the last one---the one that said there were no errors in the Bible in its original manuscripts. He then gave several reasons why it was to be despised and rejected.

1. We don't even have the original manuscripts, so how can we talk about inerrancy or lack of errors in some non-existent manuscripts?

2. We can see clearly that the Bible writers had different personalities, different vocabularies, and different styles of writing, so how could God have blocked them out and written the Bible through them? Men were the primary authors of the Bible, not God.

3. We should note that this view of dictation is a dead view as no reputable scholar holds such thoughts about the Bible today. It is the view of the ignorant and uneducated.

4. We must acknowledge that Scripture alone is the the essence of Christianity, and not some view of its supposed inspiration.

5. We must examine the character of the Bible itself, and not just twist some statements in the Bible to force the Bible to teach dictation when it does not. If we examine its character (the phenomena), we will see that it has errors in it---numerous errors of science, geography, dating, etc.

6. We must see that the great scholars of the past, including even Luther and Calvin, did not hold to any dictation idea of the Bible.

7. We must not stumble over an errant Bible, for God by the Holy Spirit is able to communicate His truth to us even through an errant book.

8. We must acknowledge that the Dictation view had done more damage to the church than any theological conviction known to man.

   a. It had divided Christians.

   b. It had convinced some simple Christians that they possessed a fullness of the truth.

   c. It had hindered true theologians from following the search for truth wherever it led them.

   d. It had made narrow-minded bigots of many people, as they thought they had the final word on every-thing because of an inerrant book.

   e. It made the "doing" of theology just a collecting of proof-texts from a supposed inerrant book, thus also discouraging real thinking whereby we arrive at the truth.

With a few more minutes left for discussion, the roof just about blew off! Everyone wanted to speak and defeat his arguments. Some were shouting and yelling! Others were fuming within, not knowing what to do. I couldn't tell if this was what the professor expected or not---it may have been getting out of hand even for him.

I felt I had to speak, so I rose to try to quiet the storm. I had to shout, "Men, men! Quiet down for a moment."

4

What Shall We Do about This Class...?

I wanted to explain to them there was a better way to handle this matter, and anyone interested in discussing the situation after class was invited to stay behind, and in a calm manner we could discuss our concerns over what we had just heard.

But with the uproar which engulfed us, it was obvious the class was over, and it would be awhile before the men would come to order. In a huff, Samuel Seavers grabbed his notes and briefcase and left the room. But that didn't stop the uproar, as everyone continued trying to talk all at once.

As I was preparing to try again to play the role of peacemaker, another man jumped to his feet.

"Men! Men! Let's quiet down and discuss this situation in a proper manner!" he suggested strongly.

"I'll never come back to this school!" one man shouted.

"Me neither! What kind of a pagan godless seminary is this anyway?" offered someone else.

"Men! Men!" the peacemaker shouted as the pandemonium continued. "Men, please, let me make a suggestion!" he offered.

When they quieted down, he made a good suggestion.

"I think we need to select a committee or team (call it what you wish), and delegate them to go see the president of the school about today's class. They can set before him the situation we faced today with the new professor."

After a few more flare-ups, this was the route the group decided to take. Several were selected, including myself and Mr. Peacemaker to visit the president. The others left while we remained to consider our strategy and complaints. To my surprise, Mr. Peacemaker didn't seem to have much complaint.

"Fellows," he said with a compassionate voice. "I think we need to be careful here. We are dealing with a new professor, and he could be very easily hurt if we don't handle this correctly. Besides, he may have just been using a teaching technique to get us stirred up to study the subject, so that theology doesn't just become to us something cold and dead."

I couldn't keep from speaking.

"I appreciate your concern for the new professor (though I don't think it is just a matter of a technique). I think the greater concern needs to be shown for the students. They have committed themselves to come to school, and someone is paying good money for a quality education, and they did not get anything that resembled that today. Our time was wasted, and our funds were ill-spent. As for myself, I have come one hundred and fifty miles one way to attend this class, and I did not and do not expect to have to sit through a tirade like that again."

"Well, just give him time," Mr. Peacemaker argued.

"No, I think we need to contact the president as you suggested in your speech during the class!" I insisted.

All the others agreed with me, and so we decided to call the president at home, and see if he would meet with us immediately, which he agreed to do. He must have hurried over, because when we got to his office he was there. Almost before we were seated, one of our group spoke up with strong conviction.

"Mr. President! Many in my rural church told me not to come to this hot-bed of liberal foolishness, and that the professors here were a bunch of blind doctors of divinity, and after this evening's class I have to agree with them. I just sat in a class where the Bible was literally ripped apart and its authority and inspiration were laughed at. What am I supposed to tell my people, and how can you expect me to come back? I'll never come back!!"

One by one, and with great emotion, my brothers spoke of the disgust for the events which had taken place in our theology class, as the president sat and listened and punctuated their speeches with phrases like, "On no!" and "You don't mean it?" and "That actually took place?" Slowly because of his seeming compassion and empathy, the men simmered down.

The thing that surprised me though was that Mr. Peacemaker, when seeing and hearing the concern of the president, changed his tune. He kept saying things like, "Yes, it was bad!" or "I couldn't believe it was taking place!" or "It sure shocked me!"

I was beginning to get a read on him, but I was not sure of the president. I concluded that a man who changes as quickly as Mr. Peacemaker might have a real problem---a chameleon problem---he changes with the environment, if it will benefit him.

Mr. President, though, was something else. He was either humoring us to calm down the situation because he was in some agreement with Samuel Seavers' doctrinal views, or he was going to fire his new professor as soon as we left. I found it difficult to think he had been involved in hiring Seavers without knowing his doctrinal convictions about such an important subject---the inspiration of the Bible. Whatever his thoughts, he did calm the storm, and he made a clear statement as to how he was going to handle the problem.

"Men, I will replace Samuel Seavers as the teacher of your class immediately. We cannot have a man teaching such things in our school! For the rest of the semester, I will be your teacher, and I promise you that you will never have to face such a hostile situation like you endured today. You have my deepest apologies for this event. I will look forward to seeing you on Thursday"

With that he was ready to dismiss us. I wanted to speak up as many questions were burning in my brain. He had not promised we would never face these views again, but that we would not face such a hostile situation. I wondered if that meant that we would face the same views in a kinder and warmer atmosphere with a more shrewd and crafty professor.

I sighed as I left the room, thinking, here we go again--- my newest doctrinal pursuit was going to be the nature of the Bible and the nature of its inspiration.

As Durwood Girvin (or his brother Samuel Seavers) might have said, my blood was running red hot for truth, my thoughts were buzzing like a swarm of bees, and my tongue was ready to strike like a scarlet snake. But I also thought, whatever I do, and whatever others do, I must act with love as clean and as pure as the starlit night!

Little did I realize how difficult that would become in this new pursuit for truth.

5

What Shall We Do about Da Dink in Dis Class...?

The late evening ride home was uneventful, except that Herby couldn't stop his fundamental marveling!

"How can a man be a professor of theology in one of our denomination's most prestigious seminarys and not believe the Bible? How could anyone hire him? That's like hiring a criminal to teach ethics, or a child-molester to baby-sit, or a fox to guard the chicken house! How could they do it?"

The only thing that stopped his raving was when we stopped at a red light and he reached over to hand a tract to someone in a car next to us. Then until the light changed, he was talking to them about Christ and His power to save sinners.

When I started forward again, here came the further expression of his bewilderment.

"How could they do it? That man doesn't believe a thing! If doctrine was clothing, he doesn't believe enough to clothe a jay bird! And how can I tell my people at church? They think every one in our beloved denomination believes the Bible. Isn't that what one would expect---that people who lead the denomination and teach in their schools would believe in the authority of the Bible!? What a crazy mixed up world this is!!"

When I arrived home, even though it was late, Terry (my wife) asked me about my day.

"Well, guess what?" I asked with a sheepish smile such as she hadn't seen in several years. But it wasn't long enough for her to have forgotten.

"Oh, no!" she exclaimed! "You've been pulled into another doctrinal pursuit. You have that look just like you had when you began the chase of the doctrines of grace, and church purity, and church government, and the doctrine of the Holy Spirit. What is the subject this time?"

I explained to her all the details of the events of the day, and she too was flabbergasted. What shocked her the most was that Durwood Girvin, or James Seavers had a twin brother, and that he taught theology at the seminary. We were still talking about it all, when I drifted off to sleep.

Though I arrived at my office a little later than usual the next morning, it was a joy to find a quiet sanctuary away from all the furor of the previous day. But not for long! Who do you suppose stopped by just as I was settling in for serious sermon preparation. You guessed it (if you have read the previous books in this series)---none other than the Dink! Dink was a converted gang leader, one of the blessings of one of our previous doctrinal pursuits.

"Hey, Preacha! How'd school go yestaday?" he queried.

When I told him the events of the day, he smiled and asked, "Preacha, does ya tink I could git in dat class? Sounds ta me like youse guys might needs some muscle in standin for da truth in dat class."

Since his conversion, he had finished a college degree. Even in his gang days, he had gotten some college credit, somewhere.

I thought he was kidding, but he wasn't, and so on Thursday there was one more rider in my car as we left town---Herby and I and da Dink! I wondered if I was going to be able to hold him down if the room exploded again in doctrinal heresy.

Again our first class was normal as before, but later after super, we made our way to the theology class with some uncertainty. The class was all situated and waiting, when the professor, Dr. Avery (also the president of the school), walked in. To our surprise, he was followed by Samuel Seavers, who took a seat in the back of the room.

"Good evening, gentlemen!" Dr. Avery began with a definite warmth and compassion already showing in his voice. "I have invited Dr. Seavers to meet with us for this semester, so that he can benefit from the teaching of this class. I trust no one has any objections."

I did have some questions, but did not voice them. For one thing, what was he to learn from the class---how to teach, or what is sound doctrine, or both? For another, why had he been allowed to stay on the faculty when he had shown such obvious views of unbelief? Could it be that he was being groomed to be able to teach the class next year, with a new more conciliatory method, but with the same heretical doctrine?

I was settling down to listen carefully and observe with precision, when Dink jumped up to speak.

"Mistuh teacha! Here's my registration stuff. I jus' enrolled taday! I wasn't here da udder day when all da theological jawin took place, so let me ask you one question before we'se begin."

I thought, "Oh, no!"

Dr. Avery looked shocked---at the language and the boldness. He probably wondered where this guy had graduated from college, but he didn't ask. He probably couldn't have gotten a word in edgewise had he tried. Dink had taken over the conversation, and no one was going to get it back till he relinquished it---and he wasn't about to do that---yet.

"I wants to ask, does ya believe da Bible ta be da livin Worda God, a divinely inspired book, and does ya believe everyting in it from cover to cover, and even what's written on da cover---Holy Bible? I'm just an old sinner saved by da grace a God, and I ain't got no time for dis class or any class unless da teacher believes dis book!! So jus' level wid me now---does ya or doesn't ya believe in dis book?"

I almost felt sorry for Dr. Avery, as he was caught totally off guard. Clearing his throat he gathered himself and began to speak, knowing all eyes and ears were on him!

6

How Shall We Determine the Nature of the Bible...?

I realized when Dink began to speak, that I should have told him to sit and listen and not say a word, but there was no stopping him once he began. I had to admit, it would be interesting to see how the professor handled the situation.

He began slowly and seemed to gain confidence the longer he spoke.

"Men, I want you to know that without a doubt I believe the Bible is the Word of God!"

A chorus of "amens!" rang out through the class room.

"It is very understandable why I should hold such a high view of Scripture, for from the time I was a child, I was taught to respect the Bible and its teachings. I can recall my father and mother reading portions of the Bible to me everyday. I would sit in awe as I listened to the recorded acts of God in history. What a joy it was to receive my first Bible when I was just a few years old. That Bible has long since been replaced by other Bibles, as each one has worn out from use over the years."

"Amens" again peppered the room during these initial statements, and I didn't want to be skeptical, but I wondered if he had really said anything of theological substance yet.

He continued with a greater forcefulness.

"I believe the Bible is the authority for the church in matters of faith and practice. The church without the Bible would be like a sailor without his compass. Church history is filled with peoples and groups that have drifted when they left the clear teachings of the Bible."

More "amens" echoed in our midst, and Dr. Avery spoke with greater strength as he continued, and as he sensed the men in the class were warming up to him. But again, I wondered what he had really said about his view of the Bible?

He wasn't finished yet.

"I believe the Bible is the authority for the individual believer as he lives his daily life. Though our culture is different from the people of the Biblical days, we can still find many helpful principles to apply to our lives to make them happier and more meaningful.

"I believe the Bible must be our doctrinal guide. Doctrinal matters can be divisive, and some doctrines are clearer in the Bible than others, but still some doctrines, especially the most important ones, come through with clarity."

I kept waiting for him to speak of the nature of the Bible's inspiration, rather than just using all the apparent orthodox clichés. My ears perked up, as in the next sentences, he began to mention revelation and inspiration.

"I believe the Bible is authoritative in the above areas because it is the result of divine revelation and inspiration. Out of God's revelation to men and inspiration of men, the Bible has come to stand for us as the testimony of the certain fact that God has spoken to men with authority. Through the Bible he continues to speak to us with authority.

"I believe the Bible needs to be preached and taught in our churches. Only by this means can men come to encounter and experience God through Christ."

With the conclusion of his statement, I noted a few "hallelujahs," and a few "praise the Lords" were heard, and all the men looked at one another nodding in agreement with his lengthy statement---all except Dink and I.

Fearing Dink might grab the floor again, I raised my hand and was recognized to speak.

"Sir, I do appreciate your statement concerning your view of the Bible. It certainly is an advance over what we heard and saw the other day. But it seems to me that your statement is rather general, and you have not stated any doctrinal conviction about the view of inspiration which you would hold. Perhaps you are going to do that now or later. But I would request that you tell us clearly what view you hold of the inspiration of the Bible."

I almost wasn't allowed to finish my question, when Mr. Peacemaker (I had found out his name was Jason Jameson) spoke up with a rather sarcastic attitude.

"What more could Dr. Avery say than what he has already stated? Pointer, are you one of those nit-picker inerrantists, who thinks God inspired the Bible in some mechanical way, by blocking out the minds, personalities, vocabularies, etc., of the Bible writers so that he could dictate the very words through them?"

I was about to answer him with grace and humility, when Dr. Avery stepped in.

"I do thank you two men for your comments, but why don't we make these questions the basis of our discussion for the next class. Your assignment, besides the reading in your textbook, is to think about these questions: Is the Bible inspired? What do we mean when we say the Bible is inspired? What is the nature of the inspiration of the Bible?"

He was ready to dismiss us, when I spoke up without even raising my hand, as I was fearful I would not be recognized.

"Sir, would not a more basic question be: How do we determine what kind of book the Bible is? Or further, how do we determine if it is inspired? Or again, where do we look to determine its nature of inspiration? Or again, where do I go to find out the nature of the inspiration of the Bible, if it is inspired?"

Dr. Avery looked a little shocked that I would ask without being given permission to speak, and I think he was shocked with the questions also. Quickly he spoke, but without some of his friendly compassionate composure.

"What do you mean by those question? I'm not following you?"

Since I had spoken without recognition, the practice continued.

"Oh, that's just nit-picker Pointer!" charged Jason Jameson.

Then Dink shocked the life out of us all when he sent forth his volley.

"He means is youse gonna go to da liberals ta find out what dey believe bout da Bible, or is youse goin to go to da conservative guys to find out what dey believe bout da Bible, or is youse gonna go to da phenomena of da Bible to determine what kind of book it is, or is youse gonna go to da Bible itself ta find out wat it says bout its own self. He means, who or what's gonna be your authority in determinin da kind a book da Bible is? Or is each man gonna decide for hisself what kinda book da Bible is out of his own thoughts or experiences?"

I thought, "Right on, Dink." But I also wondered where those ideas came from. He had cut to the heart of the question I was asking, and put it in a manner that anyone could understand.

Dr. Avery didn't seem to be very comfortable in facing the question. I don't think it was because he didn't understand it, but rather because it had focused the problem on the basic core issue---what is our authority for determining the kind of book the Bible is? But I am not sure the others in the class understood the issue, and I was afraid the question might get lost by demeaning the way Dink spoke, rather than by judging it according to the content of his speech.

Sure enough, this is what happened.

7

What More Could I Ask of His Statement...?

When the class was over, Dr. Avery asked Dink if he might speak to him a few moments. Being his pastor, I wanted to hear what was said, but I had not been invited, so I walked out with the rest of the students. Dr. Samuel Seavers had disappeared long ago, as soon as possible, at the end of the class.

As we milled around a few minutes outside the door (it was shut, so I couldn't hear what was being said), I did hear from the students some of their comments about Dink.

"Boy, who let that guy into this school?"

"How did he ever pass English?"

"How can he ever write a paper with that language problem?"

"Did you hear that long statement at the end? I'll bet he didn't even know what he was saying."

I wasn't surprised that the criticism was being led by Jason Jameson.

When Dink came out I couldn't tell if he was hurt or mad!

"What's going on?" I asked.

"Nuttin, cept he don't want me in da class! An if I am in da class, he don't want me to talk or ask questions! Whadda ya make of dat, Pastuh?"

"Well, Dink," I answered, "I could be wrong, but I think he saw that you and I were the only two he might not be able to hoodwink into believing his view point. He thought he could deal with you concerning your English, and that he can probably deal with me also if you are kept quiet. I think his goal is to say eventually the same thing that Samuel Seavers said about the Bible, but that he is going to be slow and deceptive in arriving at that goal."

"Whadda I do, Pastuh Ira?"

"You can do one of three things!" I answered. "You can change the way you speak (that will be the day, I thought to myself), or you can attend the class and keep quiet (that will be the day also, I thought again to myself), or you can drop the class."

"I ain't gonna drop no class, Preacha. I guess I'll have to keep quiet or change da way I talk."

On the way home, Herby was very quiet. He clearly was not his usual self. In fact, several opportunities to witness were allowed to pass by, something I had never seen when I had been with him, as he was absorbed in deep meditative thought. When I asked him what was wrong, he could only stutter and stammer around about being confused. When I asked if we could talk about it, he said no, but that he had to work it out by himself.

So the drive home was a slow and lonely one, as we were all absorbed in our thoughts. Dink was trying to decide what to do, Herby was confused about something, and I was sympathetic but quiet out of respect for their desires to be alone in their own contemplative thoughts.

It was still "quiet city" when I let Herby out, and then the Dink about several miles later. When I arrived home, before going to bed, I pulled out my notes and mulled over what had been said in class about the Bible. I had made a careful list of the major statements the professor had set before us. He had said the following about the Bible.

It is the Word of God.
It is the authority for the church in matters of faith and
    practice.
It is needed by the church for guidance.
It is the authority for the individual believer in his daily
    life.
It is our doctrinal guide.
It is the result of divine revelation and inspiration.
It is God's instrument to speak authoritatively to us
    today.
It needs to be preached and taught in our churches
    today.
It is the means whereby men "encounter and experience
    God through Christ."

I asked myself, as I continued to mull over the list, what was wrong with these statements? What more could be said or needed to be said---Word of God, inspiration, authority for faith and practice, by divine revelation, doctrinal guide, needed by the church and individual, and must be preached and taught so men can experience God through Christ. Those are strong words and concepts.

Was I being nit-picky, as Jason Jameson had declared, concerning Dr. Avery's statements? What more could I possibly ask him to say concerning his view of Scripture?

Yet something did not seem quite right about the situation, and I did not understand why until Sunday afternoon.

8

What Do You Believe about the Bible...?

On Sunday afternoon I attended an ordination council as practiced by our denomination, the Evangelistic Baptists. In light of the belief that every local church is autonomous and independent, it was the work of each local church to ordain its pastors (elders) and deacons.

Such ordination services were preceded by a period of examination of the candidate's life and doctrine. The examination council was held on Sunday afternoon, and all the churches of the local Baptist association were invited to send representatives to participate. The ordination service was held on Sunday evening, with only the local church and its pastors and deacons participating.

The examination of the candidate was led by an appointed moderator (usually of the candidate's choice), but the session was also open for questions by members of the council. I listened carefully for the questions (how they were stated), and the content and quality of the answers. I noticed that the questions were rather general, and the answers were rather short and shallow.

An example was the question about the Bible.

"Do you believe the Bible?" asked the moderator.

"Yes, I believe the Bible is the Word of God?" answered the candidate.

Then we moved on to the next question.

It was obvious that one could have driven a truck through the loop-holes left in his answer, yet no one said anything about it.

Not wanting to be nit-picky or obnoxious in any questions I would ask (although anything more than the simple initial questions ran the risk of that appearance), I waited until the full questioning period was over before I spoke. The moderator asked if there were any further questions.

"Mr. Moderator!" I began. "I would like to ask the candidate further about his view of the nature of Scripture. Do you, sir, believe the Bible is without errors in its original manuscripts, and that it is accurate in all matters, including history, geography, and doctrine?"

I was immediately interrupted by the moderator, who laughed and rebuked me saying, "That is a useless question, since no one has in his possession, nor has anyone ever seen the original manuscripts. How would any of us know what was in the original manuscripts, nor how accurate they were in any area? Really, do we need an original inerrant text to find the truth of the Bible? Cannot God mediate the truth to us through what we possess?"

I asked again if the young man could answer the question, and he did, as he stated, "I believe exactly what I was taught at seminary by Dr. Avery! The Bible is the inspired Word of God, given by divine revelation, and is our authority in the faith and practice of the individual believer and the church, and that it is to be preached and taught in our churches as it is God's authoritative instrument to bring men to an encounter and experience with God through Christ."

I was amazed! He too used all the "buzz" words which had been in the vocabulary of Dr. Avery---inspired, Word of

God, divine revelation, authority for faith and practice, and it is to be preached because it is God's authoritative instrument through which men encounter God through Christ. Yet I noticed that he stayed away from any idea of inerrancy---that is that the Bible is without error.

As I humbly rose to ask another question, I could sense a negative attitude from the council. I'm sure they expected what they would label as another stupid nit-picky question.

"Sir, let me ask you one more question. We all have a view of the nature of the Bible. We all have certain things we believe about the Bible, as you evidenced quite clearly and strongly in the words you used to speak of it. I would ask how do you believe we arrive at our understanding of the kind of book the Bible is?"

He replied with some confidence, and with a condescending attitude.

"By studying the phenomena of the Bible we can come to a conclusion not only of the kind of book the Bible is, but also of the kind of book the Bible isn't. Do you understand what I mean by that?" he asked with some challenge, as if he knew something I did not know, and was going to show me up.

I took his challenge.

"What other way would some men advocate as the way to judge the nature and character of the Bible?" I asked.

I had discovered in previous theological debates that many college and seminary students could mouth a position as long as it was familiar to them from what some professor had said, but they were limited in getting outside of their comfort zone of taught convictions. And I was putting before him the very issue which had been raised in the theology class---how does one determine the kind of book the Bible is?

He looked at me puzzled for a few seconds, and then he tried to dodge the question.

"Oh, I'm sure the 'fundies' have a way of arguing for their view of mechanical dictation. But anyone knows that their viewpoint of verbal inspiration is dead because of the error of equating the two. Mechanical dictation cannot account for the different personalities, styles, vocabularies, etc., found among the Bible writers. I thought we had passed the day when we thought Scripture alone was the essence of Christianity? Surely Christ is the essence of Christianity, and we need to center on Him This was certainly the view of the great reformers, as well as the great Baptists of the past."

I concluded this was not the place for a further theological debate. But I had established several convictions:

1. The use of terms in their meanings is not consistent among theologians in discussions of the nature of Scripture---that is, what I mean by the inspiration of the Bible may not be what you mean, and the same could very easily be true as we would use phrases like the Word of God, revelation, the Bible as our authority, etc. Thus, we should ask someone to define their terms in any theological discussion. And, again, it is possible for someone to use the same term and never define it, and leave the wrong impression that there is agreement in a theological doctrine between two parties when there is not.

2. Those who do not believe in an inerrant Scripture (the view known as verbal inspiration) like to set up a straw man (the idea that mechanical dictation

is equal to verbal inspiration) in order that they might defeat their opponent more easily in argumentation and debate.

3. Those who believe in an errant Scripture (the Bible has errors in its original manuscripts) make fun of those who believe in an inerrant Scripture (the Bible has no errors in the original manuscripts) insisting it is a stupid question since we do not have the original manuscripts in our possession.

4. Those who believe in an errant Scripture like to use the great men of the past to show agreement with their view, when there is some question as to the reality of the agreement of these men with their more modern concept of the Bible.

5. Those who believe in an errant Scripture like to tell us that to possess a view of inerrant Scripture slights Christ by making the Bible the center of Christianity instead of Christ.

6. Some (surely not all) who believe in an errant Scripture are mouthing a viewpoint which is only theologically skin deep. That is, they learned a view at a school, and have never thought deeply about it, nor given any other position a fair consideration (for whatever reasons prevailed upon them). Maybe the teacher never taught them the correct ideas of the opposing views. Yet with undeniable trust in their teacher, they went forth with great confidence in a position which they cannot defend, if challenged in a proper and correct manner, because their view is

shallow on one end of the debate, and built on a straw man at the other end of the discussion.

7. The candidate was putting down the inerrant view of the Bible, by referring to those who hold it as 'fundies,' which was a favorite liberal term for the 'fundamentalists,' a supposed negative reference to an older group of those who defended the verbal inspiration of the Bible.

8. The candidate did not answer my question about another way of seeking to determine the nature of the Bible besides through an analysis of the various phenomena. Those who hold to errancy hold firmly to determining the nature of the Bible by analyzing its phenomena (that is, its history, geography, etc.), and when they see some problems in these areas, they immediately conclude there are errors in the Bible. Those who hold to the inerrancy of the Bible, study the phenomena, yet are convinced that the best way to determine the nature of the Bible is to take the Bible's statements about itself and its own nature to determine the kind of book it is, including the statements of Christ, Peter, Paul and others about the clear character of Scripture.

I went home sad for the young man who had evidenced a weak view of the Bible, but certain now of Dr. Avery's view and the issues we would face in our theology class at the seminary.

I still had no answer for the Dink problem, but I soon learned he was working on it!

9

What Should We Do about Our Class at School...?

That Sunday evening I was in my study getting ready for our evening preaching service, when Dink came by. I told him all about the afternoon meeting, including the questions, the answers, and my conclusions.

"Well, den, Preacha," he offered, "we'se got it on Dr. Avery! We knows what he believes now! What do we do about it?"

I turned the tables on him when I asked, "What do you think we should do?"

"Well, da way I sees it, we'se got more dan just one problem!" he stated with some air of confidence. "We'se got my problem---do I shut up in class? An den we'se got da false teachin problem---how da we handle da error dat Dr. Avery will give us, if he believes like da preacha boy said dis afternoon at da ordination! Can we sit by an let all dose boys get indocturnated with falsehood, or is der some way we can share wid dem da truth? Pastuh, I tink even ol Herby-boy was gettin all shook up by it last week!"

"Good analysis!" I acknowledged, "but you didn't answer my question?"

"What question?" he asked playing dumb.

"What do we do about it all!"

"Well, Preacha," he began with a throwing out of his chest, as he was warming to the task now. "I's thought and prayed long and hard on dis one! I would suggest the followin. First, dat you an me both keep quiet in da class!"

"Both of us? Why both of us?" I queried with some amazement. I had figured the best thing might be for him to keep quiet, but I had hoped to counteract some of the questionable teaching by raising some solid and enlightening questions.

"Yup, I says both of us needs to shut up and let the prof talk to his heart's delight. Dat way he will become confidant to give ta us da whole wagon load of his tinkin!"

"But how do we counteract his teaching, if it is erroneous?" I spoke stating my inward concern.

"Well now, I's got da answer ta dat one too. We can have a fellowship of our own at lunch time, an invite any or all members of da class to join us in discussin da issues dat has been raised in da class!"

"You're suggesting a class to counter the real class?" I asked, playing the devil's advocate?

"No, a lunch time discussin! Who would be more pleased with young teologians talkin bout doctrin durin da lunch hour dan da president of da school---ala our professor? How could dey stop us? We's just havin a discussin of theology, and anybody is invited to come who wishes ta attend. We jus scatter da word, gets der early, grabs a table, and waits for da Lord to bring in da crowd. Den ya can lead da discussin, and I'll promise ta keep my trap shut!!"

"Me lead the discussion? You want me out on the limb by myself? What happens if someone wishes to cut the limb off on me?" I asked.

"Oh, we'll be der ta help ya---one way or anudder!" he said with a playful smile. "We won't let dem hurt ya!"

We laughed for several minutes. Then we prayed about it for several more minutes. Then we came to a conclusion.

"Dink, maybe you're right. Listen to the professor in class, and then discuss the issues out of class in a friendly lunch-time experience. Maybe it will work! We'll check it out right away! Maybe it will work!!"

With that he went on into the church sanctuary, and I was left to my own thoughts. To be honest, it was difficult to get back to my sermon for the evening. Then I had another thought---why not preach a series of sermons on the subject as we flush out the issues? Surely my people need to know of this doctrinal area also, and of the developments concerning it within our denomination.

I could hardly wait to get back to school the next week, and I wasn't too sure if such eagerness was the proper attitude for a student in the last half of the twentieth century to possess. But then again, a theological pursuit whets the appetite for serious study. But as I would soon find out, it also breeds some negative responses!---some very negative responses!

10

What Does Ya Make of Dat, Preacha...?

Before our first class on Tuesday, you would have thought that Dink was a politician, as he went from student to student, telling each one about the theological discussion to take place during the noon hour that day. I wondered how much good he was doing.

To our surprise, when we gathered in a corner in the cafeteria area, we had to put three tables together to accommodate the crowd There must have been thirty people present, which presented several potential problems.

First, would this be looked upon by the administration as some form of rebellion against authority?

Second, how would one keep out others who wished to join, even those who were not in the class, if they saw something unique taking place on campus, and wanted to join it just out of curiosity?

Third, what would keep someone or several people from disrupting the presentation and discussion, and turning it into argumentation, even argumentation of a fierce nature, and thus raise such a problem that, again, the administration would come down on us?

And then I saw another problem as I rose (I had to rise or they would never have been able to hear me). I noticed that Samuel Seavers, of all people, had joined us! What was he doing here, and who had told him of our meeting? And also, there was Jason Jameson, Mr. Peacekeeper, except when he wanted to blast the ones holding to a different view of Scripture than his.

But then too (and I don't know if this was encouraging to me or discouraging), there was old Dink, smiling and enjoying every minute of it. From his gang background before his conversion, he possessed a boldness that allowed nothing to frighten him (plus now he had the Lord to bolster him!!). I guess when you have faced knives and guns and gangsters, what were a few little, weak, snotty-nosed, neophyte preacher-boys discussing theology!

Dink may not have been afraid, but my knees were knocking when I finally began.

"Men, you all know that there is much discussion going on in the theological world today, and even in our own denomination concerning the nature of the Bible," I began slowly, loud enough for those of our group to hear, but hopefully not so loud that those at other tables could hear.

I continued gaining composure and boldness.

"Books are being written about it. Conferences are being held to discuss it. Church conventions are embroiled in debates about it. Seminaries and Christian colleges have not escaped it. Pastors are preaching about it. Laymen in some places are informed about it, while in other places, many are puzzled about it."

I spoke slowly trying to read any obvious reactions I could detect in faces or bodily actions.

"That very important something which has invaded the church scene today is the 'inerrancy debate.' The 'inerrantists' are arguing that the Bible is inerrant in its very words in the original manuscripts, while the 'errantists' are countering that the Bible has errors in the original manuscripts, though some of these don't even like to talk about the original manuscripts."

I could see by now that Jason Jameson was not happy, but I could see nothing in the face of Samuel Seavers.

"This debate has been with us for several years now, and it gives no evidence of letting up in its intensity, even in our own denomination. In fact, you probably know that at the coming national convention of Evangelistic Baptists, sides are being drawn for the election of a president, and both sides, the inerrantists and the errantists, have a candidate they are promoting. The purpose of this time of theological discussion over our noon hour each day, is to seek to understand the key issues of the current debate."

At this point Jason Jameson left, and went somewhere. His demeanor said he was not happy, so I don't think he just went to get a drink of water.

I continued.

"Each day we will seek to understand the issues of the debate, especially the inerrantist view, since that position is so often neglected or misunderstood or misrepresented, especially in academic circles. All are welcome to meet with us, but we will ask that each one who speaks or listens, abide by the common courtesies of a civilized society, and even more especially, of the teachings of our Lord."

After some time of discussion and questions of a general nature, I led them in prayer. Then I sat down, as some, who had finished eating got up to go, while others remained either finishing their lunch or talking of the session. Before I knew it Jason Jameson was in my face!

"Pointer, what are you doing? Don't you think you need some permission from the seminary officials to pull something like this? You've got about as much brass and about as little sense as your boy Dink over there! He talks dumb and you act dumb---so you two make a pretty good pair. Don't you know when you come to an academic institution that you need to put away your Sunday School thinking and become a real scholar? I don't know a scholar anywhere who holds to the inerrancy of Scripture!"

Before I could answer him he turned and started to leave, but in doing so he ran directly into Samuel Seavers, who to my surprise, dressed him down far worse than I could have or would have.

"My dear Mr. Jameson! You have a personality and an attitude as icy cold and as clammy as death! Do you not know that a list of unread books for a theological student is as convicting as a murder weapon in the hand of a suspected killer? Have you never heard of Carl Henry, or other strong advocates of the full inspiration of the Scriptures, or is your weed-clogged mini-mind incapable of even a slit of daylight from another position than your own? Come on, open your head and let a little breeze run through the cornfield of your brains, and maybe there will come some sweet perfume from both your brain and your mouth!"

And with that he was gone! I thought Jason would die on the spot, but he just gave a grunt, and then left also.

Dink whispered (something unusual for him), "What does ya make a dat, Preacha?"

"Of what?" I asked with a smile.

"Of Seavers!" he insisted.

"I make only one thing of that! God! I don't know how it all came to pass, but God somehow in His will and His way used Seavers to silence the opposition. Seavers--- the guy who started all of this to begin with---you tell me!"

Dink could only shrug his shoulders and rejoice!

11

How Do We Know What Kind of Book the Bible Is...?

After our afternoon class and supper break, we made our way back through the hallowed halls of the seminary into our evening class. We found Dr. Avery waiting for us. When he saw me come in he politely asked if I would stay after class for a few moments---he wanted to talk to me about something. Cautioning myself not to jump to conclusions, I failed to take my advice, and knew he had heard about our noon meeting, and that he would probably dress me down for my part in it.

The class itself was about what I had expected. Dr. Avery addressed us concerning how we are to determine the nature of Scripture---that is, what kind of a book the Bible really is. He used a discussion from a Bernard Ramm, and he carefully summarized it for us. The points of the lecture were the following:

1. For many years Christians have allowed the Bible to speak for itself concerning its nature, as they did in other doctrinal areas.

2. Great importance was given to systematizing the biblical witness concerning its own nature, as was also done in in the quest to systematize the Bible in every other doctrinal area. Scripture was to be the final word on every doctrine, even concerning its own nature.

Concerning this method he quoted Bernard Ramm (though Ramm did not agree with this view):

> The customary one is to read the Scriptures and pick out texts which refer to inspiration or revelation or the word of God and from these texts construe one's theology of Scripture. This has been the method of such stalwarts of this tradition as Lee, Warfield, and Gaussen. In their opinion Scripture being what it is must be verbally inspired, plenarily inspired, and inerrant in all matters of faith and fact.[1]

3. But now many modern evangelicals say we have been going about it all wrong. Instead of allowing Scripture to speak for itself concerning its nature, we must allow the phenomena of Scripture to speak to us about what kind of a book it is. He then read a another quotation from Dr. Ramm:

> The second approach is to first grasp the character of Scripture as it stands before us . . . . Viewed from Genesis to Revelation what is Scripture like in fine and in large. What is the phenomenology (i.e., careful accurate description) of Scripture? Only by a phenomenological examination of Scripture which details out the phenomena of Scripture may we adequately state the theological attributes of Scripture.[2]

Dr. Avery was virtually reading his lecture, and was somewhat unaware of what was going on in the room before him. I was listening carefully, but couldn't help but glance around from time to time to see how the rest of the class was doing. Some were staring with puzzled looks. Others seemed bored and didn't seem to care what he was saying. A few were beginning to look mad at his words.

He continued.

The careful accurate description of Scripture (phenomena) which we must use to judge the Bible (instead of the Bible's testimony itself) were the following:

1. *Scripture is history, a very special kind of history.* It is different from secular history in that its events have great theological importance concerning the past and future.

   My reaction was agreement with this statement. But I would have gone further. The Scripture certainly brings us history whose events have a great theological importance concerning the past and future. But I would add that Scripture is a divine and accurate recording of the events of history with God's authoritative interpretation of their meaning for us.

2. *Scripture is literature.* That is to say, Scripture uses all kinds of literary methods and types. Failure to recognize that could result in serious errors of interpretation.

   My reaction again was an agreement, but errors of interpretation could take place from both sides of the theological spectrum (liberal or conservatives), if one misread the method or types of literature. Conservatives are not the only ones who could make mistakes.

3. *Scripture is a revelation to man as man, and to man in his own culture.* Scripture comes to man in his language and in a specific cultural setting.

    My reaction again was agreement. But I wondered if this language was going to limit the authority and accuracy of the Bible writers due to their human and cultural limitations.

4. *Scripture is partial revelation.* It tells man something about God, man, Christ, and so forth, but not all things. It is sufficient but not exhaustive.

    My reaction again was agreement. Surely the Bible does not tell us everything about everything. Surely it is sufficient but not exhaustive. But was the author setting me up for a weakened authority and accuracy of the Scriptures?

    When Dr. Avery read the conclusions of Ramm, I saw that my suspicions were correct. I had to conclude that it is not always what someone says in a theological discussion that needs to concern you, but also what is left unsaid.
    Ramm's conclusions were as follows:

1. *The Scripture is the Word of God, but not in any infallible or inerrant sense regarding wording.*

    Thus Ramm and others of his view (including Dr. Avery, it seemed) would call the Bible the Word of God, but would see errors in it.

2. *The Scripture is the revelation of God, but again not infallible and inerrant.*

   Again Ramm and others of his view would refer to the Scripture as the revelation of God, but again this did not mean it was infallible and inerrant.

3. *Scripture is the inspired Word of God, but not in any high sense that would guarantee infallibility and inerrancy.*

   Again Ramm and others would refer to the Bible as the inspired Word of God, but with a lower understanding which would leave it as a fallible book of errors.

4. *Scripture is the canonical Word of God, but the limits of the canon are still open.*

   This means that the sixty-six books in our Bible are recognized as the Word of God (the canon), but that others could still be added to the canonical list.

5. *Canonical Scripture is the authoritative Word of God in the church.*

   But again not in any high sense of infallibility and inerrancy.

6. *Scripture is doctrinal.*

   From it we can build our doctrinal system, but we must always remember its limitations, as noted above. It is not infallible and inerrant.[3]

The class came alive when Dr. Avery looked over at me, and asked, "Well, Mr. Pointer, what do you think of Dr. Ramm's view of the Bible?"

I looked for a moment at Dink, and I thought he was going to come out of his seat. We had agreed that neither of us would speak! But we had never anticipated that the professor would ask one of us to do so. We thought he would be unwelcome to our thoughts.

What should I do? Should I tell him that Dink and I had agreed not to participate verbally in the class? If I refused to speak, would he then turn and ask Dink the same question (which could have been disastrous)? Or would Dink grab the ball by himself and run with it and tell the professor in the incomparable Dink manner just what he thought?

I decided that I had better speak up!

---

[1] Bernard Ramm, 'Scriptures As A Theological Content," *Review and Expositor* 71 (Spring 1974): 149-150.

[2] Ibid., p. 150.

[3] Ibid., pp. 154-161.

12

Who Are You to Correct a Scholar...?

I couldn't help but wonder about the motives which had prompted Dr. Avery to call on me. Was he trying to embarrass me because he was upset with me over our noon meeting? Or did he really want a conservative view, and he knew he could get one from me. I was not sure I would ever find out, but I was determined to speak my convictions concerning the truth.

"Well, Dr. Avery, please excuse me for saying it, but I think Dr. Ramm's statements give us a supreme example of the kind of evangelical double-talk which is going on concerning the nature of Scripture!"

I paused to see if he would respond so I could get a reading on him and his attitude.

Kindly, he replied, "Oh, and what do you mean by that?"

"Well," I began again with a sigh of relief at his attitude, "many are using high sounding statements with traditional conservative language when they speak of Scripture, but then the meaning of that language is undermined and contradicted by further statements and observations."

"Oh?" he interrupted. "Go on! Can you give some examples?"

"Yes," I replied, "if you will allow me to look at my notes as I answer."

I didn't wait for him to give permission, but figured he would stop me if he objected, especially since he had presented the Ramm view with extensive notes.

"Here are some examples from Ramm of high sounding language with traditional conservative words which are then contradicted by further statements."

I presented the list as given below:

"Scripture is the <u>Word</u> of God---but not fully the Word of God.

Scripture is the <u>revelation</u> of God---but not infallible and inerrant.

Scripture is the <u>inspired </u>Word of God---but not in the highest sense.

Scripture is the <u>canonical</u> Word of God---but the canon is potentially still open.

Scripture is the <u>authoritative</u> Word of God---but it only reflects the mind of God in some degree or in some measure."

"Is that all you see wrong with Ramm's view?" Dr. Avery probed further.

Dink and the rest of the class by now were sitting there on the edge of their seats with their mouths open. I couldn't stop now, so I continued.

"I think I would have to say that Ramm is inconsistent to reject Scripture's ability to speak for itself by its texts and passages concerning its nature, but then to be so positive that the phenomena can speak so authoritatively to that end. He says that the one allowing the Scripture to speak for itself has presuppositions, but then he presupposes the authority of the phenomena to speak correctly concerning the nature of Scripture, and even of his ability to analyze and interpret the phenomena with accuracy.

"Have not others examined the same phenomena and come to far different conclusions? Why should we believe his analysis and interpretation of the phenomena when other great scholars have come to opposite conclusions---that the Bible is not some special kind of history, that the Bible is not the revelation of God, that the Bible is not the inspired Word of God, that the Bible is not the canonical Word of God, that the Bible is not authoritative for the church today, and that the Bible is not doctrinal.

"All one has to do to confirm this is to read about what is called the Modernist-Fundamentalist controversy of the early part of this century. The Modernists were considered to be the greatest Bible scholars of their day, and they would have shot down every presupposed conviction of Ramm about the nature of the phenomena, and the ability of the phenomena to lead to his conclusions about what kind of book the Bible is."

"Well, Mr. Pointer! Our time is short. Could you summarize what you have said about Ramm's view?"

"Yes, I would accuse Ramm of double-talk in two respects. First, in using the strong traditional language which speaks of the nature of the Bible, but then the denial of the meaning of the words by his further statements. Seemingly he wants to be able to use all the traditional language in reference to the Bible, yet he doesn't really want to use it as historically defined. Well, he cannot have it both ways.

"Second, he errs when he seeks to convince us that his position regarding the phenomena has no presuppositions, and is therefore more capable of establishing the nature of the Scripture than the testimony of Scripture itself.

"In both instances it is a question of whether we want to follow the pathway of human reason. In the second instance, the question is, do we want to trust the ability of man to read the phenomena? Or, on the other hand, will we take the Word of God concerning its testimony about its own nature? It appears to me the second option is the correct one."

About this time, Dr. Avery was about to dismiss us, when Jason Jameson spoke up, and with some disgust and real bitterness.

"Pointer, who are you to argue with Ramm. You're just a lowly seminary student, a Bible-thumper, a would-be theologian, a mechanical dictation man, a narrow-minded 'fundy,' with a side-kick who can't even talk!"

I wasn't so irritated at him for knocking me, but I boiled when he took his shot again at Dink. To my relief Dr. Avery stepped in and closed the class. But then he made a bee-line to me, and reminded me he wanted to see me for a few minutes after class.

I had to admit that I already felt "like a fair flower disheveled in the wind," to borrow perhaps an expression from the Seavers boys. I hoped it wouldn't take long. I was tired and it had been a long day, and we still had a long drive home!

13

Will You Teach the Class Next Time...?

As I waited for the class to clear, I reviewed in my mind what I knew about Dr. Avery. He appeared to be a kind man, yet he was not one who believed in the inerrancy of Scripture. He had denied Dink the privilege of speaking in class, but was that for his benefit or Dink's? That is, had he been trying to protect Dink from some of the proud, ivory-towered airheads of seminary life who had no concern for a young Christian, especially one who was not of their elite status? Was he going to chew me out, or was this going to be a cordial meeting.

Finally my questions were answered, as the last student cleared the room, and we were left alone. His first statement surprised me.

"Well, how did it go today in your noon meeting?"

"I thought it went well," I replied. "There was a good crowd, more than expected, and there was a strong interest, and there was order among those who attended. I was very encouraged."

"What is the purpose of these meetings?" he queried.

"To stir theological discussion, for one thing, and to be honest, to give the conservative viewpoint a fair shake for anyone who wants to hear it," I replied.

"Then it is a conservative meeting?" he asked again.

"Well, yes, since the non-conservative view gets sufficient exposure in class, we just wanted to be balanced in spreading ideas at a school, which I am sure, praises and desires academic freedom." I declared, knowing the strength of the last phrase.

"Didn't you ever think to ask the administration for permission to do this?" he continued.

"Yes, but we concluded that since we were just a bunch of students meeting over lunch to discuss theology, there would be no real opposition from the administration, unless we handled it improperly, or it got out of hand, or it became divisive," I answered honestly.

"Well, Mr. Pointer, I'll tell you what I am going to do. I am going to approve of your meeting on those conditions--- that your meeting not get out of hand and become divisive. I don't hardly see how I can stop the honest discussion of theology on a seminary campus. But believe me, you had better keep it in line and not let it degenerate into name-calling, or bitterness, or divisiveness. Do you understand that?"

"Yes, sir, I do understand that, and I will do my best to keep it under control. But will you not admit that sometimes things can get out of control from the non-conservative students, even in a classroom setting, and even when it is led by a teacher?" I declared, remembering the class we had just concluded.

He smiled.

"Touché, brother, if you're referring to Jason Jameson and his ignorant tirade at the end of our class. I guess every viewpoint has ignoramuses in their midst!"

I smiled, knowing I had seen in the past and would probably see some more conservative ignoramuses even in the area of the defense of the nature of Scripture.

"Oh, one more thing! Would you teach the class next time we meet, and present the reasons you are convinced we must let Scripture be our authority in every area of doctrine, including our doctrine of the nature of Scripture? You might do a better job of it than I would, seeing that is your conviction."

I readily agreed, although I did not know when I would get time to prepare the study.

And with that we parted, but my day was not yet over. As Dink, Herby and I walked to the car, I found Samuel Seavers waiting for me in one of the crevices of the campus. He requested that the other men go on, but asked if we could talk for a moment.

"My dear brother Pointer! You probably think I am a man caught in the web of a labyrinth of perplexities, one who in his actions is incapable of giving any clear and coherent statement as to his loyalties in this battle for the Bible."

I had to admit, his actions had puzzled me. He was a flaming liberal concerning the Bible in our first class, and then today he had stifled Jason Jameson in the noon meeting.

He went on.

"Someday I will explain to you what must and will in the future appear to be an infinite series of illusions or contradictions. I may very well in these days ahead present you with many breathless nights and days of suspenseful and pondering mystery in my words and actions. But trust me, for I know what I am doing, and all will be made clear then, and you will agree with and appreciate my actions."

With that he turned and was gone before I could ask any questions. I was glad as we got to the car that I was not driving. It gave me opportunity to rest my mind, and rethink, as best I could, the events of the day.

14

What Shall We Do with the Liberals...?

My mind was frazzled as we made our way home, but nonetheless, I began thinking how I would teach the class on Thursday---especially difficult since this was Tuesday.

Dink's continual jabber didn't help either, but finally the conversation was confined to him and Herby, as I appeared to be dozing. I was really organizing my thoughts for the next challenge. Then I remembered it was not the next challenge, for I would need to lead the noon meeting on Thursday as well.

When I arrived home, though it was late, I tried to fill Terry, my wife, in on everything (did I say everything?). Well, I did the best I could do before falling off to sleep, with the promise I would finish the story tomorrow. This I did at breakfast, while I also got reacquainted with Ira, our only child, who was now over three years old.

Though it was a little later than normal for my leaving the house to go to the church office, I didn't think anyone would disturb me at the house. But unexpectedly there came a knock at the door.

Reluctantly I went to the door, and there stood Todd Shelton, my old college friend who over the years had chased, so it seemed, every extreme doctrinal viewpoint that had raised its head in his pathway. His wife, just three or so years ago, had left him, partly due to his instability. He had been out of the ministry for those years, and I had seen much less of him than before, which was not too bad an idea for me.

"Well, I hear you've got them going up at seminary!" he declared with a laugh.

"Who told you about it?" I asked, but then realized that was an unnecessary question.

We both answered at the same time, "Da Dink!"

"Do you think I can get in that class?" he asked with a sheepish grin. "And do you think I could ride with you all?"

I gave a sigh of frustration, but I didn't think he noticed it. All we needed in the present mix was unpredictable Todd.

"You'll have to ask the seminary that. It may be too late to register. How can you go to school, anyway? You're working a secular job," I declared again.

"Not any more! I am now a pastor again. I was called just Sunday to a great church in Bangleville---the First Baptist Church. That's not too far from seminary. They said I could attend classes, if I wished!"

"You could drive from Bangleville---its not that far!" I firmly suggested.

"Yeah, but look at the fun we could have!" he chuckled. "And I could help you in the doctrinal battle for the truth!"

"Well, you check it out, and then meet us at school, and we'll talk about a ride and all the rest," I said ending the conversation. I really hoped he was just windy, and come Thursday would have changed his mind. Maybe I should have just prayed for the wind to change its direction.

As we gathered on Thursday for lunch, sure enough, there was old Todd!

"Ira, if you need any help handling this luncheon meeting or the class, just let me know!" he offered.

I didn't know whether he meant leading or teaching or what. I thanked him, and then called our group to order. There were more present than had attended the first meeting. I passed out the outline sheets I had prepared, and then we began.

"Last Tuesday at this noon meeting, we said we wanted to seek to understand the inerrancy debate, and so today we would like to give you a brief historical overview of where we are today in that controversy. But in order to do that, I need to give you some historical background.

"If you will go back to the turn of this twentieth century, you will remember that a prevalent conviction of that day concerning the Bible was the 'old liberal view.' This position held the Bible to be an inspired book, but its inspiration was no greater than the other great books of history, such as the writings of Shakespeare. The higher critical method of Biblical scholarship of the nineteenth century, had pretty well ruled out the possibility of any supernatural aspects of the Bible as being true and acceptable. This view had tested the date, authorship, language, style and chronology of each of the Biblical books, and had concluded that the Bible was not written by the men traditionally recognized as the authors, nor was it written according to the previously accepted dates."

Much to my dismay, one of the stalwart conservative boys just had to speak up.

"They should have strung up those godless liberals from the closest church steeple!" he cried.

"Now men, I would ask you to keep your comments to yourself. We are here to understand, and not condemn. And we will be allowed to meet like this only as long as we meet with a proper attitude and with the absence of such comments---from either side," I warned.

Silence prevailed once again, so I continued.

"Plus you only interrupt our thought process and ability of understanding!" I challenged, as I struggled to pick up my own train of thought.

"It was further concluded by this old liberal view, that the Bible in many places was little more than the patchwork of an editor or several editors, as they pieced together, so the scholars claimed, various manuscripts. Obviously, though they liked to refer to the Bible as an inspired book, they did not believe it was supernaturally inspired by God. Rather they were convinced it was the work of man---the best that man could offer in his understanding of religious matters. In the telling of the narration, the Biblical writers had spiced the Bible with an abundance of legends, myths, and folklore."

Time was flying, so I summarized the remaining material as follows from my outline, with a few comments:

The foundations and beliefs of the old liberal view

a. The higher critical method of analyzing the Bible which possessed a very strong anti-supernatural bias (what we had already covered).

b. The theology of evolution which held a high view of man and his capabilities and the following ideas and beliefs:

   1) *Man is not the direct creation of God--- he is the product of blind evolutionary forces.*

   2) *Man is not a fallen creature.*

3) *Man did start low but by the process of evolution he is climbing upward.*

4) *Man will soon by his own power bring a utopia on earth.*

5) *Man is perfectible and capable of bringing perfection to all things, including himself.*

6) *As man has progressed through the years so has his knowledge, and therefore a book like the Bible, written years ago, could not be the final authority for the advanced man of the present age.*

7) *Christ is not a Redeemer from sin, nor does he possess the attributes of deity, but he is a human example for us to follow in our upward quest and journey.*

8) *The work of the church is not the salvation of the individual by any message of atonement, but the improvement or salvation of society by the message of love and morality.*

My time was up, so I had to close. I explained we would continue our historical survey next week. The crowd quickly scattered and left me standing putting material back into my briefcase.

When I looked up I was shocked at who was standing in front of me!

15

Who Is the Strawman...?

As I lifted my eyes from my briefcase, I flinched, because standing there almost eyeball to eyeball was a giant scarecrow-looking figure. Obviously it was someone dressed up in something that resembled a Halloween costume.

Whoever was pulling this prank began screaming, "Strawman! Strawman! Strawman! Pointer's building strawmen!"

With those words, the creature turned and ran out of the dining area, I guess, to wherever he had come from. I smiled and made my way to the afternoon class, wondering what kind of joke had just been played on me.

Was it just an innocent prank, or did it reveal that someone was very serious in their dislike of what we were doing at the lunch hour? Or were they trying to unnerve me for the evening class I was supposed to lead later? Since he had entered after every one else had scattered, there was no one left to follow him to determine his identity or residence.

As we gathered for our afternoon class, the professor noted there were several more enrolled for the class, than there were at the beginning. In calling the roll, the only one absent was Jason Jameson. But he too came dragging in just as the teacher was finishing his introduction of the subject. I must admit these events raised the question in my mind if Jameson was the scare-crow figure that had faced me in the dining hall.

Later in the evening class, which I was teaching at Dr. Avery's request, I began by passing out an outline of my presentation. I, then, set forth our problem.

"The question before us is this: How do we know what kind of book the Bible is? There are two possibilities before us.

"First, there is the newer approach which says we must look at the phenomena of the Bible to determine its nature. That is, we must look at the Bible as it stands before us, and ask what the external attributes of the Bible tell us about its nature. These phenomena, we have been told in our last class, show us the Bible is as follows:

1. Scripture is a very special kind of history.
2. Scripture is literature.
3. Scripture is revelation to man as man, and to man in his own culture.
4. Scripture is partial revelation.

"But when we read these phenomena, we come to the following conclusions about the Bible:

1. Scripture is the Word of God, but not in any infallible or inerrant sense regarding wording.
2. Scripture is the revelation of God, but again it is not infallible and inerrant.
3. Scripture is the inspired Word of God, but not in any high sense that would guarantee infallibility and inerrancy.
4. Scripture is the canonical Word of God, but the limits of the canon are still open.

5. Canonical Scripture is the authoritative Word of God in the church, but not in any inerrant sense.
6. Scripture is doctrinal, but limited in its ability to form doctrine, especially any doctrine of the nature of Scripture."

I couldn't help smiling at this point, and saying with some friendly sarcasm, "Isn't it amazing what some can see about the Bible from reading the phenomena."

Then I turned to the other view.

"Second, there is the traditional method of allowing the Bible to speak to us of its nature, as we would take the words of the Biblical writers (even men like Paul and Peter) and the Biblical characters (even Christ Himself) to inform us of the nature of the book we call our authority.

"And I don't mean to over-simplify the issue, but is it not a question of taking what modern scholars say about the Bible from trying to read the phenomena as opposed to taking what Christ and the Biblical writers said about the Bible and its nature? Would you prefer what Ramm says about the nature of Scripture or what Christ says? Would you prefer what I say about the nature of Scripture or what Paul says?

"That is the heart of the issue, and so now we turn to see what Christ said about Scripture. Did He say to read the phenomena of God's Word as it stands before you, or did He testify concerning the nature of Scripture directly?"

Thus I began to quote several verses, making brief comments concerning each. I could see that Jason Jameson was not receiving my comments.

It is written, Man shall not live by bread alone, but by every word which proceedeth out of the mouth of God.
Matthew 4:4

1. In each of the three temptations Christ faced, He quoted an Old Testament verse to defeat Satan:

   Deuteronomy 8:3 quoted in Matthew 4:4
   Deuteronomy 6:16 quoted in Matthew 4:7
   Deuteronomy 6:13 quoted in Matthew 4:10

2. If anyone says that Christ is not referring in this verse to the Old Testament, when He refers to words which precede out of the mouth of God, that one is violating the context of the passage, for that is exactly what Christ does---He does not live by bread but by the Word which precedes out of God---the verses He quotes from the Old Testament to defeat Satan in the temptation.

3. It is also interesting to note that as Christ used the Old Testament as His authority in these verses, that Satan had no accusation to raise against the Scripture at any point in the conflict.

4. As one notes Satan's methods in the Bible, it is to be seen that he can quote Scripture, he can misapply and misinterpret it, or he can appear to believe it to get his way. But in this passage he does not attack the authority or reliability or trustworthiness of Scripture. Surely if there had been one flaw in Scripture, he would have

pounced on it in his battle with Christ. But he could not stand in the presence of the eternal Son of God and raise one objection concerning the nature of the Word of God. That tactic worked years before in the garden of Eden with Adam and Eve, but he knew it would not work with Christ.

5. Why didn't he chide Christ for believing:

   a book full of errors?
   a book with historical slips?
   a book with geographical contradictions?
   a book with chronological uncertainties?
   a book which was a patchwork of various
       documents by unknown editors?

6. Why did not Satan criticize Christ for saying that every word of God is authoritative?

   Man shall live by every word which comes
       from the mouth of God
   Is this not verbal inspiration? The Bible is
       inspired to its very words!
   Is this not plenary inspiration? The Bible
       is inspired to every word! (plenary
       means whole or all)

My time was running out, and I had spent most of it on this one section of Scripture. So I quickly commented on the other words of Christ about Scripture, including Matthew 5:18

*For verily I say unto you, till heaven and earth pass,
one jot or one tittle shall in no way pass from the law,
till all be fulfilled.*

Verily---this means Christ is speaking the truth!
The Law here refers to the OT Scripture!
The jot refers to the smallest letter of the
    Hebrew alphabet!
The tittle is another small portion of the
    Hebrew alphabet!
The jot and tittle shall not pass away in the
    Scripture till all is fulfilled.
Thus the truth Christ stresses is as follows:
    the authority and accuracy of Scripture extends
        not just to the ideas of Scripture
        not just to the letters of Scripture
        but even to the letters and parts of the letters
But even further Christ's negation is emphatic
    these jots and tittles shall <u>not</u> pass away
        it is a double negative in the Greek
    thus these jots and tittles and letters and words
        shall never ever under any circumstance
            at any time
            at any place
            in any manner
        pass away till all is fulfilled
Is this not plenary verbal inspiration?

Though I had more verses from Christ, and others from Peter and Paul, I had to close the hour of study. I simply added, "Men, you can believe who you wish to believe, but I think it is clear whose testimony I would take concerning the nature of Scripture."

As I sat down, the class applauded enthusiastically. One student requested that Dr. Avery give me the next class hour to finish my presentation, and he agreed. In fact all agreed, except Jason Jameson, who walked out threatening to leave the seminary for one with some scholarship.

16

Does Verbal Inspiration Equal Mechanical Dictation...?

When we approached Herby's car for the drive home, we didn't notice anything wrong till he had started the engine and turned on the lights. There staring us in the face were some twisted windshield wipers. We jumped out of the car to examine them more closely, and we found that someone had bent them away from the windshield in a grotesque fashion, while leaving them still fastened to the arm which controlled them. We tried to twist them back in shape, but found it was impossible.

Thus we drove home, grateful to the Lord it was not raining, with weird shaped wipers reminding us that someone had pulled another prank on us. The question was, were these two pranks, the Strawman and the wipers, related and the act of the same person, or were they separate events? Perhaps a more practical question was, how much would it take for Herby to get new wipers? We all agreed that we would share the expense, whatever it was.

The remainder of the week was rather uneventful, except for study and normal pastoral ministry. My mind was constantly on the next Tuesday's presentations. On Saturday I prepared, having finished my messages for the Sunday services, the Tuesday luncheon material. The outline set forth the following.

The Fundamentalist View of the Bible

Introduction
1. A brief review of the old liberal view
2. The spread of the old liberal view from Germany to
    the USA at the turn of the century
3. The influence of the old liberal view in the USA
    it captured many of the leading
        denominations
        Christian colleges
        seminaries
        pulpits
4. The rise of the fundamentalist view of the Bible
    this was not a new view
    it was the traditional view responding
    to the old liberal view

I   THE FUNDAMENTALISTS' CONVICTIONS ABOUT THE BIBLE

A. <u>It was a view of verbal plenary inspiration</u>

    the Bible is the divinely inspired Word of God
        its inspiration extends to the very words
            of the Bible
            in the original manuscripts
        the Bible writers wrote as led and controlled
            by the Holy Spirit
        thus the Scriptures bore the characteristics
            of revelation and of inspiration
        thus inspiration and revelation
            were not just the possession of the authors
            but of the very manuscripts themselves

B. <u>It was not a view of mechanical dictation</u>

mechanical dictation says
>that the Holy Spirit wrote through the writers
>>as one would write on a typewriter
>>as one would play a musical instrument
>that is the writers were passive in the operation
mechanical dictation is easily defeated
>by the opponents of verbal inspiration
>by pointing out the presence
>>of the varying vocabularies of the writers
>>of the varying personalities of the writers
>>of the varying styles of the writers
but verbal inspiration is not mechanical dictation
>this idea is only a straw man built by opponents
a true understanding of verbal inspiration says
>the Holy Spirit spoke through human writers
>the Holy Spirit used their varying
>>styles
>>personalities
>>vocabularies
>the work of inspiration was
>>the perfect union of the human and the divine
>>with the Holy Spirit guiding the authors
>>>to the proper words
>>>and keeping them from any kind of errors
>the result was an inerrant manuscript
>>in the original script

I closed the study with this long summary statement:

Those who would conclude that verbal inspiration is dead and is to be rejected because it equals mechanical dictation have erred in that they have examined the wrong corpse. Their whole case is built on the presupposition that verbal inspiration equals mechanical dictation. When the wrong body (mechanical dictation) is examined, it is easily seen to have a serious ailment---the problem of differing styles and vocabularies in the Bible.

On the other hand, when the right body (the proper understanding of verbal inspiration) is examined, there is no such problem. In simple words, verbal inspiration does not equal mechanical dictation. Mechanical dictation is a straw man set up by the opponents of verbal inspiration so that they may easily defeat the doctrine of verbal inspiration.

But there are similarities between verbal inspiration and mechanical dictation. Both see God as the author of Scripture. Both acknowledge man as the agent involved in inspiration. Both agree that the result is a perfect and infallible text in the original manuscripts. Both hold that the words and truth of Scripture are inerrant.

On the basis of those similarities, many have concluded that the two are equal. To reach such a conclusion demonstrates a failure to distinguish precisely one's categories of thought. It shows also an unawareness of the scholars who have set forth carefully a proper view of verbal inspiration.

The crucial difference between the two is on the matter of the balance between the human and the divine. Mechanical dictation overbalances in the direction of the divine. A perfect book is the result, but at the expense of man's full involvement. The varying vocabularies and styles of the writers are by-passed---God simply used the writers as passive tools, as a man would use a typewriter. However, a proper understanding of verbal inspiration fully balances the human and the divine, and yet produces a perfect text as the result. God, by His full power, used man in his full powers and thereby guaranteed a perfect text

As I was finishing preparation of my presentation, the phone rang and a strange sounding, deep, slow-speaking voice addressed me.

"P-a-s-t-o-r P-o-i-n-t-e-r? T-h-i-s i-s t-h-e S-t-r-a-w-m-a-n! I a-m a-l-s-o y-o-u-r f-r-i-e-n-d-l-y w-i-n-d-s-h-i-e-l-d w-i-p-e-r r-e-p-a-i-r-m-a-n! H-a --- h-a --- h-a!! A-r-e y-o-u r-e-a-d-y f-o-r n-e-x-t T-u-e-s-d-a-y??"

And then he hung up.

One question had been answered. Whoever this Strawman was, he was also responsible for the vandalism on Herby's windshield wipers.

But who was he? And what was his purpose? Was he trying to discourage us from presenting a conservative position concerning the nature of the Bible? And would he stop just at boyish pranks, or was he capable of more dangerous and threatening actions?

I had a lot to think about as I realized, that in my pursuit of truth, I may well have become the pursued.

17

Who Was Karl Barth...?

As we drove to the seminary the next Tuesday, I filled Herby and Dink in on the phone call from the Strawman. Dink was ready to use physical force to find out who this strange character was. He was convinced it was Jason Jameson.

"Didja notice how dat guy came in late after da appearance of da Strawman in da cafeteria? Who else came in late? Who else could it have been?"

Herby then suggested another possibility---Todd Shelton!

"I know Todd's a friend of yours, Ira, but this never happened till the day he came to campus for the class. And besides, he came in late that day also, saying he had been delayed by registering for the class."

Knowing this was all premature, and that the evidence was very partial, I urged them both to keep their eyes open, and maybe the Lord would expose this fellow to us in His time.

The luncheon period went well, as we presented and then discussed the idea that verbal inspiration does not equal mechanical dictation. Todd and Jason were both there, as was the biggest crowd yet. In fact it was so large, that we were granted permission to meet in one of the side isolated areas in the future, which meant we would have much more privacy behind closed doors.

But another problem was building. Some of the other students and even some of the faculty were beginning to protest what we were doing. They had gone to Dr. Avery, the school president, with their complaints. I didn't know then what he had told them, but no one had stopped us yet. In fact, the permission to meet in one of the side reserved areas seemed to indicate we had some backing of the administration. But I must confess that I wondered why also.

In the evening class I continued with the history of the current inerrancy controversy. We had covered previously the old liberal view at the turn of the century, and then the response of the fundamentalists who defended the verbal inspiration of the Bible. We were now ready for the next step---the emergence of Karl Barth and neo-orthodoxy.

I passed out the following outline, and began moving through the material.

I   THE BIBLE STOOD IN SHAMBLES BECAUSE
    OF THE OLD LIBERAL VIEW (Early 20th c.)

It was nothing more than the best that man could offer.
It possessed no authority.
It contained no certain "Thus saith the Lord."
It actually was not needed as a basis for Christianity.
It was not possible as a basis for Christianity.

II THE BIBLE WAS RESCUED FROM THE
    LIBERALS BY KARL BARTH

    A. Who was Karl Barth?

       he was the son of a liberal German professor

he went forth to preach but had no Bible to preach
he realized he had no authority from God
he became convinced that the Bible was needed
he could/would not return to verbal inspiration
    his liberal training had ruled this out
he could not though remain a liberal
    for the above reasons
he seemed hedged in with no place to go

B. <u>What did Karl Barth do to rescue the Bible from the liberals</u>?

Barth moved the characteristics of revelation
    from the Bible itself (verbal inspiration)
    to the writers' experiences
the old liberals had taken the character of revelation
    away from the Bible and the Biblical writers
        the Bible writers were just men
        writing the best they could on religion
the view of verbal inspiration had seen the Bible
    as revelation
    because the Biblical writers
        had been inspired by divine revelation
    and because also the Holy Spirit
        had guided them as they wrote
        which gave the Bible the character
            of revelation also
but Barth removed this character of revelation
    from the Bible
    to place the character of revelation
        in the experience of the writers

At this point I had to add a few explanatory paragraphs.

Thus according to Barth, the Biblical writers had revelational encounters or experiences with God, but the content of such revelational encounters could not be put in writing with any kind of full or complete verbal accuracy or in any completely truthful propositional manner. These Biblical writers recorded a human witness to their divine revelational encounter or experience with God. Therefore one must not be surprised to find errors in their writings---geographical, scientific, historical, chronological or theological errors---because the Bible is only a human witness of the real revelation---the encounter that the writers had with God.

I noted that several valid questions rise at this point.

1. What good would such a Bible be in the preaching and teaching ministry of the church?

2. Can a Bible full of errors be an instrument of God for the accomplishment of His work?

Barth would answer, yes. The Bible becomes an instrument of authority for preaching and teaching, even though it has errors, by the power of the Holy Spirit. Because it is the human witness of the revelational encounter, the Holy Spirit can use it to give men of today an encounter with God. The Holy Spirit, it seems, works a miracle and makes the Bible become the Word of God to us as He desires. As the Bible stands in its propositional form before us, it is not the Word of God. But as the Holy Spirit makes the Bible come alive to us, it becomes the Word of God for us. From this understanding there comes the oft-quoted definition of the neo-orthodox view (another name for Barth's convictions)---the Bible contains the Word of God.

Barth's view of Scripture swept the religious world of his day. He was considered something of a hero by many. He had saved the Bible from liberal destruction. He had given men a reason to preach the Bible. Few seemed to care that in the process, his view still left a Bible full of errors and had robbed the church of propositional truth, which, it seems to me, was too great a price to pay. Many schools and denominations that had survived the old liberal view were now touched deeply by the new Barthian concept of revelation. But really the church was no better off than she had been under the old liberal view. The destructive convictions of theologians was now easier to disguise and thereby it was easier to deceive the lay people concerning the fact that their views of the Bible were not really orthodox.

I stopped at this point for some discussion, waiting for someone to attack me on that last statement. The class seemed to be in strong agreement, except for Jason Jameson, who had scowled at me during the entire class time.

"That's not what I believe about the Bible! I'm not an old liberal, and I'm not a Barthian. And I certainly am not in agreement with mechanical dictation!" he declared emphatically, still using the phrase "mechanical dictation" to refer to verbal inspiration.

"I realize that you and many others are not Barthian. But I think you have been influenced by Barth's theology!" I declared. I was prepared for a few more sentences, when Dr. Avery interrupted.

"Why don't we continue this discussion in our next class? Mr. Pointer, would you lead us again, and tell us what you think Mr. Jameson and others, perhaps including myself, believe about the Bible?"

I agreed and was rather surprised that he wanted me to lead another class, in light of the rumbling which was beginning to show itself over the campus concerning our noon meeting. What would these people say when they heard I was teaching several classes on the subject, and in the class of the president?

My question in this area was answered after class as Dr. Avery asked me to remain for a few moments of discussion! I did, but I suggested to Dink and Herby that they go check our car and guard it till I got there.

18

Will You Help Us Find a New Faculty Member...?

When the room had cleared, Dr. Avery approached me and spoke with some caution and quietness.

"I know you have been wondering about my allowing the noon luncheon and your participation in this class. And I know that it is stirring some opposition on and off of campus. I do apologize for any difficulty it may have brought to you, or that it might bring to you in the future. But I have a reason for what I am doing."

He kept looking at the door, to see if anyone was there who might see us talking or even hear what we were saying.

"My reason for allowing you such freedom to present a position with which I do not agree, and a position with which most faculty members do not agree, even though it brings controversy on the campus, is because of the greater controversy on the subject off the campus."

I assumed he was referring to the controversy taking place in the denomination, and I was certainly fully aware of those rumblings. There was a real battle going on between the conservatives, who believed in verbal inspiration, and the moderates (they preferred this name to liberals), who did not. It seems the moderates had been in control for years, though they showcased the conservatives as presidents, and though the denomination was at its grass-roots conservative as well. The moderates didn't care if the conservatives had some key positions, as long as they had control of the agencies, schools, and primary organizations of the denomination.

The moderates had taken control of these agencies, etc., by positioning their people on the controlling boards. And though the presidents had authority to appoint the nominating committee, which presented names to the annual denominational meeting of those to serve on the boards of the agencies and institutions, some of the conservative past presidents had admitted (with some apology) that they had done little more than rubber-stamp the names given to them for service on the convention nominating committee.

Now, however, the conservatives had come alive, and they were seeking to elect conservative presidents, who would appoint conservatives to the nominating committee, who then would nominate conservative trustees to the boards of the agencies and schools (including the seminaries). This meant that in time the boards would be conservative, and that they could turn the agencies and schools back to a conservative position. This was being seen as a threat by the present faculty members and administrators, and it seems clear now that the same was true, in this case of Dr. Avery, who was a moderate seminary president.

Dr. Avery continued.

"The question is being asked, and it will be asked more and more, if we have an academic freedom here that allows the conservative viewpoint to be presented. I hope you do not think I am using you, Mr. Pointer, but your emergence has given an opportunity for a clear presentation of the conservative viewpoint. I know what I am doing may be looked upon as purely political by the conservatives, and as pure compromise by the moderates. So I am in an almost no-win situation. But I do appreciate you and the help you have given me in this battle."

I must confess, I had some mixed emotions over the whole situation. I now realized that I too was in the middle of the battlefield. I was helping the conservative cause by being able to do what I was doing, but I was also helping the moderates to appear to be doing something that they had seemingly refused to do before the pressure of the denominational controversy---that is, to allow the conservative position to be taught with an openness and fairness. And he had said I was helping him (a moderate seminary president) to do something he had not been willing to do before.

All kinds of questions shot through my mind. Was he doing this to save his job and to keep the seminary under moderate control in the future? Would he have done this if the denominational controversy had not erupted and threatened the moderate utopia which had been built at so many denominational schools and seminaries?

Then he hit me with another question which seemed to be of the same nature---that is, to satisfy the pressure which was upon him.

"We're interviewing a prospective faculty member in about a week, and we would like to include you in a student group that would participate in that meeting."

I sure had a question on that request!

"Is this an open session? That is, can I ask him any question I wish? Or will I just be some token conservative on the committee who will be treated rudely with moderate disdain if I ask about his view of the Scripture?"

He smiled as he answered, "Not much gets by you, does it, Mr. Pointer? I guarantee you that it will be a fair and open discussion."

"Who will be in charge to keep it that way?" I asked.

"I will be there and will moderate the session. We will do it over lunch one day. You might have to make a special trip to the seminary, but knowing your passion over this issue, I think you will be glad to be there."

"And who else is on this committee of students?" I asked, still maintaining a somewhat skeptical attitude.

He blushed and hung his head as he replied, "Well, mostly upper classmen."

"Why only upper classmen? Is it that these men are ones who have been influenced towards the moderate view, and will give a positive recommendation to hiring another moderate?"

"You've got me there!" he admitted. "You probably are right. We have seemed to operate that way in the past. Probably we should change that approach now. We've justified it by declaring this could best be done by upper classmen who are more mature in their thinking than the first or second year students, which was correct, but I see now it did not represent both views."

"And what will be the outcome of our meeting with the candidate?" I asked again, trying to anticipate every situation.

"What do you mean?" he asked.

"Will this committee make some decision to recommend or not recommend him as a faculty member?"

"Yes, it will." he declared.

"Will one dissenting vote ever be heard by the trustees or anyone else?" I queried again.

"Well, I'll tell you what I'll do! If you are the one dissenting vote, I will let you come to the board meeting of the trustees when his name is presented, that is, if he passes all other criteria and interviews, to state your objections."

I didn't answer him on that one. I told him I would come to the meeting, and see how it went, and then decide about this final request.

"Can I ask you one more question, Dr. Avery?" I asked.

"Certainly!" he affirmed, probably not dreaming what would be next.

"How long has it been since you have considered a conservative for a teaching position here at the seminary?" I fired, as kindly but as direct as I could."

Then I added, "You really don't have to answer that question, and I do apologize if it seemed too caustic."

"No," he countered, "It was a fair and proper question, and I am ashamed to say it has been a long, long time."

Then he added with a smile, maybe just to flatter me, "If you had a doctorate, maybe we could consider you!"

Then he became very pensive as he spoke.

"Or if I were younger, maybe I would be that man. You know, Pointer, I used to be a strong conservative, and I must admit that your presentations have unexpectedly warmed my heart these past few days! I wish I could believe that way again."

When the discussion was over, I headed for the parking lot. I had driven my car that day, and had wondered through the day the fate of my car, since that was the place the Strawman had struck last week. When Herby and Dink saw me coming, they began to yell.

"Ira, wait till you see what he's done to your car."

19

What Is the Essence of Christianity...?

As I walked towards my car, with Herby and Dink yelling at me about what had been done to it, I just hoped it was nothing to disable it. I was tired and wanted to get home. But no such providence.

As I got closer, I could see they were pointing to the front part of the car, and that the headlights had been knocked out. And the same was true of the tail lights! There was no way we could drive home now!

Also, scrawled across the hood was a message:

Roses are red,
Violets are blue.
For punishing the heretics,
Call Strawman, please do!!

As we were wondering how we were going to get home, Jason Jameson came strolling upon the scene. He appeared to be very sympathetic (the most friendly we had ever seen him to be), but one wondered if it was the criminal returning to the scene of the crime. I also pondered if his friendliness was some sort of sadistic glee over our predicament. And then he even offered to drive us home. We had no choice, so we agreed to his offer.

During the trip home, all was fairly silent, until Jason offered a bit of information (or was it lies he gave us?). He told us that he had been by the parking lot earlier in the evening and had seen Todd Shelton coming away from the car. He said Todd had looked rather suspicious and was evasive when he asked him what he had been doing there. He said he then walked over to the car and saw the damage. He knew we would need a ride home, and that's why he came back about the time he thought the class would be over.

The rest of the way home I wondered if Jason could be trusted to tell the truth, and why all of a sudden he was "Mr. Nice Guy" to us. The next morning, a Wednesday, I called back to Seminary City and made arrangements to get my car fixed, so we could pick it up on Thursday, our next class day. The rest of the day I was scurrying to take care of pastoral matters in the morning, and then, finally, in the early afternoon I settled in for study in preparation for the Thursday sessions.

I decided in the noon study to deal with the question of the essence of Christianity. The moderates, I had discovered, were accusing the conservatives, who held to the inerrancy of Scripture, of making the Bible the essence of Christianity rather than Christ.

I would begin with a quote from Ramm with a notation that the word *Wesen* in his quote means "essence:"

One's doctrine of Scripture has become now the first and most important doctrine, one's theory of the *Wesen* of Christianity, so that all other doctrines have validity now only as they are part of the inerrant Scripture. Thus evangelical teachers, or evangelical schools or evangelical movements, can be judged as to whether or not they are true to the *Wesen* of Christianity by their theory of inspiration. It can be stated even more directly: an evangelical has made a theory of inspiration the *Wesen* of Christianity if he assumes that the most important doctrine in a man's theology, and the most revelatory of the entire range of his theological thought, is his theology of inspiration.[1]

I tried to summarize the main ideas of Ramm's statement.

1. Not stated here, but clear in Ramm's thought is that Jesus Christ is the *Wesen* (essence) of the Christian faith---the essence of Christianity.

2. If one assumes that the most important doctrine in a man's theology is his theology of inspiration (no doubt a reference to those holding to inerrancy or verbal inspiration), he has ceased to allow Christ to be the essence of Christianity. Rather a view of the Bible has become the essence of Christianity.

3. Not stated, but nonetheless a logical conclusion from Ramm's statement, is that one's view of the nature of the Bible is not too important---the important issue and the essence of Christianity is Christ.

I noted several thoughts concerning the Ramm quote:

1. That I would have to commend Ramm for pointing out that the essence of Christianity is Christ. Yes, definitely, the essence of the Christian faith and doctrine centers on the person and work of Jesus Christ. Positively, this is the core of the gospel that must be proclaimed to a lost world. This

gospel is the power of God unto salvation,
not one's view of Scripture.

2. That I would have to take issue with Ramm for his
    failure to see a crucial relationship between
    the doctrine of biblical inerrancy and the *Wesen*
    (essence) of Christianity.

3. That the reason many conservatives of today are
    so concerned about upholding the doctrine of in-
    errancy is not because they wish to make that
    viewpoint the essence of Christianity, but because
    they perceive clearly a relationship between in-
    errancy and the *Wesen*.

4. That for many conservatives, the battle with liberal
    theology early in this century points out such a
    relationship and demonstrates the loss of the
    essence of Christianity, when the doctrine of biblical
    inerrancy is rejected.

5. Agreed, the battle with old liberalism is past and the
    situation is quite different today. Nonetheless, the
    battle provides us with an important lesson. It was
    no accident that the old liberal view came to a denial
    of the deity of Christ, His substitutionary death, and
    even His resurrection---these denials were the
    logical outcome of its low view of Scripture.

6. That though this is a different day, and though the
    denial of the full authority of Scripture does not
    seem to be as severe as the old liberal view, the
    modern view of errancy of Scripture brings to the

conservatives of today a very deep concern which the errantists do not seem to want to recognize or admit.

7. That these concerns can be stated by the following questions:

    a. Is it consistent to hold to biblical authority and yet deny biblical inerrancy?

    b. Will not this view of denying inerrancy while seeking to uphold biblical authority lead us to a greater subjectivity in interpreting the Bible, even the eventual loss or change of the essential doctrines of Christianity?

    c. Can the moderates today, who hold to an errant Bible, guarantee that the succeeding generations of their scholars will also hold to the essential doctrines of Christianity from the foundation they have championed?

    d. Is it not proper to seek to defend biblical inerrancy because of a relationship that exists between the doctrine of Scripture and the essence of Christianity?

    e. Is it really logical to say that we believe all the evangelical doctrines of the Bible while denying the foundational evangelical doctrine of the full and absolute truthfulness of the Scripture?

  f. Is it consistent to deny the full authority and absolute truthfulness of the Bible in its own statements about itself, but then claim to be able to use the same Bible to set before us in an unerring manner the essential doctrines of the faith?

  g. Or to put it another way, is it consistent to hold all the essential doctrines of the faith of evangelicals (which are based on the testimony of the Bible), and yet at the same time deny the testimony of the Bible about itself?

My conclusion was that that there is a relationship which exists between the doctrine of Scripture and the essence of Christianity. A weak and erroneous foundation of authority cannot give a clear understanding of the essence of Christianity.

And that conviction does not make the doctrine of the inerrancy of Scripture the essence of Christianity any more than a concern for a clean hospital operating room makes that the essence of surgery!

My thoughts were interrupted by Todd as he walked into my office. Now I could ask him about his presence at the scene around the time my car was trashed!

---

[1] Bernard Ramm, "Is 'Scripture Alone' the Essence of Christianity?" in *Biblical Authority*, ed. Jack Rogers (Waco, Texas: Word, 1977), pp. 109-23.

20

Do You Think I'm the Strawman...?

"Hey, Ira, my old scholarly buddy!" Todd exclaimed with his previous exuberance. I could only wonder what brought him to my area. He lived towards Seminary City.

"I'll bet you are wondering what I am doing down here, aren't you?"

I admitted that had been and continued to be my first thought, when I saw him come through the door.

"Well, I've brought you your car!" he exclaimed with great pride and expectancy, so it seemed, of my appreciation and thanks.

I explained that he didn't have to do that, but he continued to be very magnanimous in his attitude, which made it very difficult to ask him the question about the trashing of my car. But I figured I would give it a shot anyway.

"Todd, what do you know about the damage done to my car the other night?" I asked in a subdued manner.

"What do I know? Nothing!! Absolutely nothing!" he proclaimed.

"Well, Jason Jameson says he saw you coming away from the car, and when he went to the car he saw it had been damaged. Were you there, and did you see the damage, and did you see Jason there also?"

"Whoa, what is this---the inquisition?" he protested.

"No." I explained. "I'm just trying to gather information in a quest to find out who this Strawman is!"

"You don't think I am the Strawman?" he protested even louder.

"Right now I don't know who the Strawman is! I'm just trying to gather information, and all I can see is that you are somewhat hesitant, so it seems, to give me any answers," I said directly.

"Well, for your information, its just the opposite! I saw Jason coming away from your car, and he acted suspicious when I asked him about your car! If you ask me, he's the Strawman!"

"Todd, what were you doing there?" I asked trying not to offend.

"Hey, I was just walking by! Any law against that? Is this the thanks I get for bringing you your car?" he spoke rebukingly.

With that he marched out muttering to himself. Efforts to stop him failed, so I let him go. I had not intended to hurt him, and I did wonder if he protested too strongly when interrogated. Maybe he was the Strawman.

Then about ten minutes after he was gone, guess who called! He spoke in the same low and slow voice.

"S-o h-o-w d-i-d y-o-u l-i-k-e y-o-u-r c-a-r, M-r. P-o-i-n-t-e-r? I-t s-e-e-m-s y-o-u l-o-s-t y-o-u-r l-i-g-h-t-s! O-f c-o-u-r-s-e, b-e-l-i-e-v-i-n-g a-s y-o-u d-o, y-o-u d-i-d-n-t h-a-v-e m-u-c-h l-i-g-h-t t-o s-t-a-r-t w-i-t-h! A-n-d I h-e-a-r y-o-u t-h-i-n-k t-h-e S-t-r-a-w-m-a-n i-s J-a-s-o-n J-a-m-e-s-o-n o-r T-o-d-d S-h-e-l-t-o-n? K-e-e-p l-o-o-k-i-n-g a-n-d j-u-s-t m-a-y-b-e y-o-u-'-l-l f-i-n-d m-e! I a-m c-r-e-a-t-i-n-g q-u-i-t-e a s-t-i-r o-n c-a-m-p-u-s, a-r-e-n-'-t I?"

And then again, he was gone. I had kept listening, trying to pick up something in his voice or inflection of words, or even his vocabulary that would help me identify him. But I found nothing. The most interesting statement was about creating a stir on campus. It was clear that he was enjoying the attention and mystery he was creating. There was one other question: How did he know that we suspected Jason and Todd of being the Strawman?

Thursday morning came quick and early, especially following that busy Wednesday, including the evening prayer and study service. I did have my car to drive to Seminary City, but Dink insisted on driving his. He had rigged up some alarm systems that would discourage anyone from attempting damage, as his alarms would let the whole world know if anyone tried something.

The noon discussion on the essence of Christianity went well. But as I faced the evening class, probably for the last time, something happened right after the lunch hour, which made it clear the evening session might be difficult!

21

Who Is in the Phraseological Quagmire...?

Following my noon presentation, I was approached by Samuel Seavers, who seemed desirous of facing me with a challenge.

"Mr. Pointer! I am sure you are aware, that I, who was brought here to teach your evening class, have been forced to languish in obscurity, while a man without a seminary degree has been pontificating with stale and facile platitudes. Surely my days have been stamped with unutterable and solemn woe, when I had expected to soar and bless like the sweet smoke of burning twigs hovering in an autumn day. I want you to know that in tonight's class, I will not sleep in my rosy zone of contemplation, but I will arise again as the supreme arbitrator of the conduct of my class!"

I had no idea of how he could fulfill this threat, but I soon found out that evening. When I arrived for the class, I was informed by Seavers himself, that Dr. Avery was absent for that night, and the class had been turned over to him! He was superintending the class for the coming hour!

All began well! I had wondered if he was going to be nasty in introducing me, but he was very kind and gracious, even the exact opposite of his attitude in the cafeteria. So I took over after his introduction, and began, still wondering when he would carry out his threat.

I first gave the class some review.

I   THE BIBLE STOOD IN SHAMBLES ACCORDING TO THE OLD LIBERAL VIEW

It was nothing more than the best that man could offer.
It possessed no authority.
It contained no certain "Thus saith the Lord."
It actually was not needed as a basis for Christianity.
It was not possible as a basis for Christianity.

II THE BIBLE WAS RESCUED FROM THE LIBERALS BY KARL BARTH

A. Who was Karl Barth?

he was the son of a liberal theological professor
he went forth to preach but had no Bible to preach
he realized he had no authority from God
he became convinced that the Bible was needed
he could/would not return to verbal inspiration
    his liberal training had ruled this out
he could not though remain a liberal
    for the above reasons
he seemed hedged in with no place to go

B. What did Karl Barth do to rescue the Bible from the liberals?

Barth moved the characteristics of revelation
    from the Bible itself (verbal inspiration)
    to the writers' experiences
the Bible for Barth was the human witness
    of these revelational experiences of the writers

the Bible does not contain propositional truth
but is only a human statement
about experiences of revelation

I then reminded them of the question we faced as the class had ended. How is Barth different from moderate evangelicals today? I outlined the material as follows:

I   THE PRESSURE OF THE VIEWS OF BARTH ON THE CONSERVATIVES OF HIS DAY

A. Barth's view brought pressure on young theologians of his day

1. <u>a number of these young conservatives</u>

traveled to Germany
to study with him
or to study with one of his disciples

2. <u>some used the excuse</u>

that they were going to learn how
to combat Barth's theology
but they failed to realize
how compelling and persuasive and powerful
the Barthian view was
especially in an arena where other views
such as verbal inspiration
were not even considered
a possible option for a scholar

B. Barth caused many young conservatives to jump
    the inerrancy fence

    1. <u>they did not follow Barth in his total scheme</u>

        that the Bible is the human witness
            of the revelational encounter
            of the Biblical writers

    2. <u>but they concluded that</u>

        they could no longer defend verbal inspiration
        they had to acknowledge errors in the Bible
        they still could believe
            in all other evangelical doctrines
            of the Bible

    3. <u>thus for them</u>

        parts of the Bible are inerrant
        and parts of the Bible are errant

    4. <u>they had various ways of identifying these parts</u>

        some said
            the doctrinal parts are inerrant
            the non-doctrinal parts are not
        some said
            the thoughts are inspired
            but the words are not inspired
        some said
            the revelational parts are inspired
            the non-revelational parts are not

5. these are the ones who develop their view of
    inspiration from the phenomena of the Bible
    rather than from the testimony of the Bible

II THE PROBLEMS CREATED BY THESE NEW ERRANTISTS

The switch from inerrancy to errancy by these
conservatives leaves many problems in its wake.

1. Does it make sense to declare the revelational
    parts of Scripture, which cannot be tested, to be
    inerrant, when one has already concluded that
    non-revelational parts, which can be tested, can
    be shown to have supposed errors?

2. Does the errantist have a way of determining
    which part of the Scripture is errant and which
    is inerrant, even under the various supposed
    categories listed above? Does not human
    reason become authoritative in this process?

3. Does the Bible ever give us such an understanding
    of Scripture, or is it the influence of the unbelief
    of the Enlightenment which has allowed such
    thinking?

4. Does not this practice, method and belief breed
    an uncertain theological system, which in turn
    will breed an existential (experiential) system
    of hermeneutics (principles of interpreting the
    Bible), which will in turn breed an uncertainty
    in the pulpit?

5. Will not much more be changed if we reject
    the doctrine of inerrancy, such as methods of
    evangelism, methods of building the church,
    the method of sanctification of the believer,
    etc., as men reject the teaching of the Word
    in favor of the methods and practices of man?

6. How can these new evangelicals expect those
    who are committed to the inerrancy of Scripture
    to accept them and recognize them and labor
    with them in the body of Christ? Yet that is
    what is expected!

At this point I was interrupted by Samuel Seavers.

"All right, Mr. Pointer! You have sent forth your weak pictures and dream-like images, along with a few flashes of witty irrelevance, in your own indescribably reckless and desperate manner long enough. Let me for a few moments rescue you from your phraseological quagmire."

He then proceeded to tell us that the view I had just sought to demolish was the view of the great reformers, Calvin and Luther. They, he said, were the evangelical errantists of their day. If he thought I had bored the class into a "phraseological quagmire," mine was nothing compared to his. When the bell sounded, he still droned on.

When he finally let us out of class, we all agreed that he had done the position he was defending more harm than good!

We headed for the car to see if any damage had been done to Dink's car. At least, none of the alarms had gone off---yet.

22

What Is the Strawman Coming to Now...?

As I made my way to the car, I continued to ponder the strangeness of Samuel Seavers. I guess I shouldn't have been surprised, since his brother, James, had been one of the most puzzling and unpredictable characters I had ever met.[1] I tried to categorize what I knew about him.

I noted in my mind that he had done the following: He had trashed the Bible in the first theology class. He had been removed as teacher by the president, Dr. Avery. He had rebuked Jason Jameson for making fun of the conservative position, something he had already done himself. He had listened rather quietly at the noon sessions and the classes as I taught. He had now tried to humiliate me in front of the class. And then I remembered his statement to us, that we would not understand him until later, but bear with him, and some day he would explain his actions.

What a strange bird he had turned out to be!

When we arrived at the automobile, we discovered that all was well, except that when we ourselves tried to get in, we set off a couple of the alarm systems Dink had hooked up. How embarrassing it was to stand there as eyes emerged from everywhere to gawk at us, wondering what was going on. Finally, Dink got them under control, and we started out the seminary drive, looking forward to getting home.

But as we came to the end of the drive, a shot crashed through the window of the car! And then a second one! We all jumped out into the dark and took cover, with Dink yelling into the darkness at whoever was shooting, that the gunman wouldn't have gotten away with this if Dink had brought his gun. The blood of an ex-gangster, like Dink, boils quickly when someone is shooting at him.

After some moments it was quiet again. I told Dink I was going to sneak back to a telephone and call the police. When the police arrived, they took our report, and said they would investigate. And we headed out the seminary gate for home.

A few blocks away from the school, I suggested that we pull into Handy Andy's Hamburgers for something to drink. I was exhausted, tired and dry. As we pulled up, we noticed something very unusual. Inside the restaurant we saw Todd Shelton and Jason Jameson. We could only see that they were laughing about something. We wondered if their being together, and their laughter had anything to do with the shooting that night. They didn't notice us until we walked in the front door.

When they saw us, they looked rather sheepish and quite surprised.

"We thought you guys would be long gone down the rode to Collegetown!" Todd began.

"No," I explained, "something happened again tonight to detain us."

"Did somebody puncture your tires tonight?" Jason asked with a giant laugh.

"No, someone tried to kill us!" I shot back, not very happy to make a joke of the whole ordeal.

"What?" Todd queried. "Tried to kill you? Who would do that?"

"We dunno!" offered the Dink. "Whoever tried dat had better hope we'se never finds out who dey is. We tought it might be youse guys!" he challenged, as his blood began to boil again.

"Us?" asked Todd with some fear, because he knew Dink and what his previous life had been. "You've got the wrong guys! We've been here ever since class was over!" he declared.

Then Todd and Jason got out of there.

"There's one way to find out if they have been here very long!" I nodded to Dink and Herby. "We can ask the waitress."

When we did, she said they had been there about fifteen minutes, and that seemed clear also from the fact they left their glasses of milk shakes half full. We had been with the police for about an hour. Could it be that we had two Strawmen---Todd and Jason? But if so, what had brought them together? And to shoot at us? They could have killed one of us!

We got something to drink, and got on the road for the ride home more puzzled than ever over this unfolding mystery. All of it, so it seemed, was over one's view of the Bible. What in the world are professing Christians capable of in a doctrinal battle? Who would have or could have believed it?

But the worst was yet to come!

---

[1] See a previous book in this series, *A Journey in the Spirit*, by the same author, published by Richbarry Press (1997).

23

Who Do You Think You Are...?

The rest of the week was overwhelming in its plain old commonality. Nothing new, nothing unexpected, nothing too difficult---just pastoral ministry! What a relief!

Then on Monday, I had to make the trip back to Seminary City for the meeting with the prospective faculty member. I was not sure how this all would go, or what my responsibility was, exactly, but I went trusting in the Lord.

We met for lunch at a local restaurant, one of the more elegant ones in town. The group consisted of Dr. Avery, the prospective faculty member, named Dr. William Post, and four students, all upper classmen except myself.

As the lunch began and continued, I kept waiting for someone to ask him questions, since that seemed to be our job. Surely we were not there just to find out if he was a nice guy with whom to have lunch. I realized others of the seminary, such as a faculty committee, and, probably others, would interview him, but I had been given the impression by Dr. Avery that we were to interview him also.

Finally the dessert was served and no one had said a thing except to get acquainted with him---his family, his hobbies, etc. There had not been a single doctrinal question asked. When it seemed to be winding down, and Dr. Avery asked if there were any other questions (I hadn't seen very many of substance yet), I spoke up. I wanted to ask several questions, but figured I would have to be satisfied with the most basic one---what did he believe about the Bible.

And so I began, not knowing what to expect from the candidate, or the students present, or even Dr. Avery.

"Dr. Post, could I ask you what your position is on the nature of Scripture?" I began with some timidity of heart but with a straight-forwardness in my voice.

He was very congenial as he replied, "Oh, I believe the Bible is the Word of God."

I got the feeling he thought that would suffice, and that the rest of the group thought the same, but I had come a long way, and had been promised I could ask questions, and had been told I was not just a token conservative, so I tried again.

"Well, sir, excuse me, if I ask the question again. Many people could use the phrase 'I believe the Bible to be the Word of God,' even Karl Barth, so could I ask you to elaborate for us?"

"The Bible is our record of the revelation of God!" he declared emphatically as if he were miffed at me for asking again. "It is the Word about God, it is the Word from God, it is the Word to reveal God, it is the Word to fulfill the purpose of God, and it is the Word whereby we encounter the truth of God."

I knew I would anger him more, and even irk my fellow students if I asked again, but I did not care. I had an assignment and I had to carry it out.

"Sir, again, please excuse me. You have spoken as if you hold a Barthian or an errancy view. Let me ask you very directly: Is the Bible inspired in the sense that it is the infallible and inerrant Word of God in its original manuscripts? Or to put it another way, would you agree with the statement that God has revealed himself in history, and that revelation has been recorded in a verbal and plenarily inspired, inerrant and infallible Bible in its original manuscripts?"

It was obvious he was not pleased with my further questions, and I braced myself for his answer, but all I got was a set of questions.

"Young man, what year are you in this school?"

When I told him I was a first year student, he threw back his head and laughed me off saying, "No wonder you are asking such ignorant and shallow questions. I suppose you can tell us where the original manuscripts are!"

I had wondered before why many of these moderates would not answer questions, but instead want to run down the questioner, his motives, or his position by the use of a strawman.

He continued with his questions.

"Who do you think you are to ask me these questions? Do you have the years of education which I possess? Have you taught at the distinguished schools where I have served? Have you authored books on theological subjects as I have?"

I glanced at Dr. Avery, and I could tell that he was not happy with the way I was being treated, especially since he wanted a truce between the various views, along with his desire for peace on the campus, and in light of the fact he had invited me for this very purpose---to ask questions.

My adversary was not finished.

"Young man, you are as the troublers of Job, who wished to accuse him as he was in the midst of his suffering. They thought they knew it all---all about God, and all about His ways. And you appear to think you know it all---all about how God gave us His truth, and all about who ought to teach at this school, and who should not. Our denomination would be better off without the likes of you."

I interrupted him with a smile.

"Sir, though you have not intended to, you have answered my question and shown me more than I asked. I know now what you believe about the Bible, and I know your attitude towards those who do not agree with you. I know also that you are not interested in discussing theological questions in a gentlemanly manner, but wish to dominate and insult those who do not agree with you. I wonder why you cannot tell me your view of Scripture in a straight-forward and understandable manner? I am sorry, sir, but I could not recommend you to teach at our school."

He shot back, "If there are more students like you at your school, I am not sure I would want to teach there either." And that ended our discussion.

Obviously the rest of the time together was tense, and we soon scattered. As we left the restaurant, Dr. Avery called me aside and apologized. He was a true gentleman. He told me I had handled myself well, and that I had asked proper questions, and that I had kept a kind attitude even when the discussion turned sour. He said he sympathized with me if I was left shell-shocked and disturbed by the events which had just unfolded. He acknowledge that he was ashamed of the way some of his colleagues acted on this subject.

I was shell-shocked to some extent, but sometimes thats the price one pays for standing for the truth. Truth does have its price. Ask Jeremiah, or Isaiah, or Daniel, or Jesus, or Paul. We seem much better sometimes, at extolling our heroes, than being willing to imitate them.

24

Where Are the Original Manuscripts...?

I had decided to spend Monday night in Seminary City, in light of the immediate return for classes early Tuesday morning. I checked into a motel, and then went over to the campus to use the library for preparation for the noon meeting. My days of teaching the class were finished, and, to be honest, I was glad.

On the way to the library, I saw something strange, something I had seen once before, but only on a class day. As I turned into the campus, I saw Todd and Jason sitting together on a bench, talking with great concentration---so much was their intensity that they didn't even see me. I went around and parked behind some buildings, but when I came back to where they were sitting (I had to in order to get to the library), they were gone.

I had three questions (only because of the Strawman incidents---otherwise it was none of my business). What was Todd doing in town on Monday, and what were they doing together, and did their meeting have anything to do with the Strawman?

The next day at noon, I sought to present an answer to the oft-asked question, "Where are the original manuscripts?" I was beginning to get the impression that it was a question of ridicule. I presented the material from the following outline, noticing that Todd and Jason were present---even smiling at me.

I   THE QUESTION OR OBJECTION STATED

How can one argue for the inerrancy of the original
   manuscripts---
         when we do not possess them?
         when we therefore cannot examine them?
         when we have never seen them?

Does not common sense preclude
   that one cannot make a judgment
         concerning that which he does not possess?
         concerning that which does not exist?

Is it not a prerequisite that one examine these originals
   to determine their nature and character
   before one makes statements about their inerrancy?

II   THE QUESTION OR OBJECTION ANSWERED

A. The real problem here

   The problem here is the failure to distinguish
         between *total evidence* and *sufficient evidence*
         and between the use we make of each.

   The demand for the original manuscripts
         before we can believe in inerrancy
         is a demand for total evidence.

B. An honest admission here

   It must be admitted that such total evidence
         does not exist---it has not been provided us.

Scholars differ regarding how close our copies come in equalling the originals---but no competent scholar would argue that we possess the originals or that anyone has reconstructed perfectly the original text with a one hundred per cent equality.

C. A strong argument here

a. *Total evidence is not needed in other matters of our doctrinal beliefs*

We do not have total evidence for any of our doctrinal commitments.

Example---We do not have total evidence for the existence or character of God. Such would demand that we be able to see God in order to examine His character and nature. But God is a Spirit, and that negates any possibility of total evidence for His existence. Yet, we still believe in God. As Christians we have a life and death commitment to Him even though we do not have total evidence for His existence. Our hearts even break for the atheist or agnostic who demands total evidence before he acknowledges the existence of God.

Conclusion---If we do not have total evidence for the existence of God, and yet believe He exists, does that mean we have only a blind faith? No, rather we believe in His existence on the basis of sufficient evidence. We accept Scripture as authoritative, sufficient evidence concerning the existence, nature, character, and attributes of God.

Example---We do not have total evidence for any doctrinal truth. Where is the total evidence for the Trinity? We believe the doctrine of the Trinity because of the clear testimony of the sufficient evidence of the Scripture. Where is the total evidence for the doctrine of creation? or of the doctrine of the incarnation? or of the life of Christ? or of the death of Christ? or of the bodily resurrection of Christ? or of the miracles of Christ? Total evidence before we would believe these truths would demand we be able to examine all of those on a firsthand basis. But we cannot! Yet we accept these doctrines on the sufficient evidence of the Scriptures.

b. *The demand for total evidence (the original manuscripts) before we would believe in the doctrine of inerrancy is unnecessary in its practice and inconsistent in its logic.*

Because we accept the sufficient evidence of the Scripture rather than total evidence for our other doctrinal beliefs, it is only logical for us to accept the sufficient evidence of the Bible concerning its own nature and character.

> It is inconsistent to waive the necessity of total evidence concerning all other doctrinal matters and then to turn around and demand that we possess total evidence concerning the nature of Scripture itself.

> If we deny the ability of Scripture to speak authoritatively concerning its own nature, then we must also question its ability to speak with full authority concerning all other matters of doctrine.

CONCLUSION

Therefore, the question is not, "Do we possess the original manuscripts?" but, "What does the Scripture say about itself."

I closed by reminding them that we had seen the testimony of Scripture concerning itself in one of our class sessions, and that it does teach inerrancy.

Immediately when I was finished, Jason and Todd were in my face!

"We know who the Strawman is!" Todd whispered, but with great exclamation.

"Who?" I asked. "And what is the evidence?"

"We'll tell you after class!" they said, quietly mouthing their words again, as they turned quickly and scurried from the cafeteria.

25

What about Luther and Calvin...?

As I was headed for class, and walking alone through the campus, suddenly Samuel Seavers stepped out in front of me from one of the bushes. He beckoned me to come over to him, where it was not so obvious that we were talking to each other.

"I thought you might be interested to know that the name of the Stawman burns in my mind now like a gray and illuminating candle flame---there are actually two of them!" he stated with assurance.

"Todd and Jason?" I asked, creating a puzzled look on his face.

"How did you know?" he asked, not using any flowery language.

"Well, just two minutes ago, they told me they knew who the Strawman was!" I admitted.

"Who did they say he is!" he demanded now.

"They didn't say! They said they would tell me later," I explained.

"I know what those scoundrels are going to do as they toy with you like a child trifles at play! They are going to accuse me of being the Strawman! Well, till the sleep of death steals upon me like a burnt out candle, I will not let them get away with that!" And he too turned abruptly and departed.

I must admit that the Systematic Theology class that night was a little boring, though I was interested in the subject. My mind was more occupied on the identity of the Strawman. I was going to corner Todd and Jason after class and ask them to identify him for me. And I would get the evidence from them as well!

Dr. Avery spoke on the views of Calvin and Luther concerning the nature of Scripture. He said of Luther, "You cannot separate Luther's view of the Bible from his view of Christ. For him, only Christ was without error. His faith was in the content of the Scripture, not in its errancy or inerrancy. When Calvin used words and phrases and statements which seem to say he believed in inerrancy, Dr. Avery said he was not speaking about absolute accuracy in every part, but of the ability of the Bible to perform God's work in us, especially to bring the message of the righteousness of God to us."

I summarized in my notes what he had said about Luther's view of the Bible.

1. Christ alone is without error.

2. Luther's faith was in the content of Scripture, though it has error, but nonetheless reveals an inerrant Christ.

3. Luther did use words which seemed to indicate an inerrant Scripture, but he meant that the Bible was capable of revealing the inerrant Christ to us for the performance of God's work of His righteousness within us.

4. One must reinterpret any words which Luther spoke which seemed to indicate that he believed in an inerrant Scripture.

He went on for quite awhile, trying to explain away Luther's statements concerning the Bible. I wanted to ask how we could have faith in the content of the Bible, when it came to us in such an erroneous manner---in words that were full of error? But I kept still, thinking I would honor my original agreement with Dink---if he could not speak, then neither would I.

When Dr. Avery turned to Calvin, he did little better. He stated concerning Calvin's view that "Because all men have an innate knowledge of God which is suppressed by their state of sin, God has given a better way of knowledge, that is, the revelation of Scripture. But we must not elevate the Scripture above Christ! For Calvin, the central thesis of Scripture is Jesus Christ, and the primary purpose of Scripture is to reveal Christ to us in a salvific manner, even though the message of Christ comes to us through imperfect words."

I summarized in my notes once again what Dr. Avery had said about Calvin's view of the Bible.

1. All men have an innate knowledge of God which is suppressed by their sin.

2. God has given man a better way of knowledge, therefore, and that is the revelation of Scripture.

3. We must be careful not to elevate the Scripture above Christ.

4. The primary purpose of Scripture is to reveal Christ in a saving way, and we must not demand any kind of inerrancy in Scripture in order for it to be able to do that.

When the class was over, and as I was leaving, I made it a point to try to confront Todd and Jason, but Jason was already gone.

"Well, give me the information and the evidence!" I insisted.

"Brother Ira," Todd stated again in whispers. "Samuel Seavers is the Strawmen. Shh! Watch how you react."

"It might interest you to know, that he says you and Jason are the Strawman!" I volunteered, waiting for a reaction. "Now where is your evidence against him?" I insisted.

"In time, my friend. In time...." he said as his voice trailed off and as he trailed away also.

I was tired, and eager to get on the road towards home, but almost like every Tuesday, the day was not over yet!

26

Where Shall I Spend the Night...?

As I made my way to the car in a dark parking lot (I was driving home alone since I had stayed over night), I was a little cautious. Dink and Herby had gone, and I was pretty much in no man's land as I cut through the darkness to my vehicle.

Suddenly someone came from the shadows and knocked me to the ground with a glancing but painful blow to the head. Then he stood over me threatening me. I could see enough to observe that he was dressed as the Strawman, and that he had a tire iron in his hand. His first blow had been strong enough to daze me and convince me not to try anything. He spoke in the same elongated slow deep drawl.

"I d-e-m-a-n-d t-h-a-t y-o-u s-t-o-p t-h-e n-o-o-n s-t-u-d-y, a-n-d a-t-t-e-n-d n-o m-o-r-e m-e-e-t-i-n-g-s i-n r-e-f-e-r-e-n-c-e t-o f-a-c-u-l-t-y i-n-t-e-r-v-i-e-w-s o-r i-n r-e-f-e-r-e-n-c-e t-o a-n-y-t-h-i-n-g t-h-a-t h-a-s t-o d-o w-i-t-h t-h-e p-r-o-m-o-t-i-o-n o-f i-n-e-r-r-a-n-c-y o-n t-h-i-s c-a-m-p-u-s. I-f y-o-u d-o n-o-t h-e-e-d m-y w-a-r-n-i-n-g, y-o-u w-i-l-l b-e s-o-r-r-y."

As he disappeared into the darkness, I tried to get to my feet, but his blow left me stumbling and spinning in the off-balanced fashion of an alcoholic or a child at play doing the windmill. I dropped to one knee to get my head out of the whirly-gig city to which he had assigned me, and by the time

I was even half-way back to normal and capable of pursuit, it was too late.

I stopped by Handy Andy's Hamburger joint for something cold to drink, thinking that might refresh me and clear my head for the drive home. I tried to relive the encounter with the Strawman, and suddenly I realized something. The voice! It sounded different in some way! I reminded myself that I had encountered him tonight in person, while previously his messages had come by telephone. Maybe that was the difference. But there was something else about the voice! It was not as deep, nor was the drawl as pronounced, nor was the voice as slow as on the phone.

I wondered if this was evidence that there were two Strawmen, Todd and Jason. When I had spoken to Todd, just before walking across campus, Jason was already gone. He would have had time to dress as the Strawman and get in place to confront me. Maybe they were taking turns playing the Strawman.

On the other hand, maybe it was Samuel Seavers trying to deceive us and make us believe his claim that there were two Strawmen. Maybe he had changed his voice intentionally in order to implicate Jason and Todd. Thus my conclusion was that the difference of voice could be the ploy of either side to bolster their claims.

I got up from the booth, and started towards the car, and the whirly-gigs invaded my head once again. I knew I couldn't drive home. I had only one decision to make--- would it be another night in Seminary City in the motel or the hospital? The more I tried to walk and discovered I couldn't, and the more the pain pounded my brain, the more I became convinced it had to be the hospital. Wait till my wife hears about this, I thought, as someone called an ambulance.

The next morning I looked up from the hospital bed, and Dr. Avery was standing beside me.

"Mr. Pointer! What happened to you? Is it true that someone beat you up on campus last night---someone everyone is calling 'Strawman?'"

Best I could in my still painful condition, I told him what had been taking place regarding the Strawman episode. He said he had heard of the Strawman's original appearance at the noon luncheon, but figured it was just a prank of some student. But he said he had not heard of the shooting, and he was very upset that no one had told him about it.

"How did you learn about my assault by the Strawman last night?" I queried. "You must have heard about it late last night or early this morning."

"He called me and told me about it!" he declared.

"He---the Strawman himself?" I asked. "Did you recognize his voice?"

"No, it was very deep and rough and with a slow drawl. It could have been anyone! Who do you think it is?" he asked.

"Well, Jason and Todd say its Samuel Seavers, and Samuel Seavers say its Jason and Todd. I have no idea who it is, do you?"

He laughed, and then apologized for laughing, in light of my plight. Then he said jokingly, "Next, they will be accusing me of being the Strawman!"

I laughed back and responded, "Well, I guess the only one you can rule out is me! I've been attacked by him twice, and he's called me on the phone several times."

27

Will You Give Me an Interview...?

After Dr. Avery had left, the thought flashed through my mind---could he be the Strawman. No, I told myself---not in a million years!

That afternoon they released me from the hospital. They had decided it was just a mild concussion, and so, to keep from driving home, I went back and checked into the motel. I called Terry (I had called her from the hospital the evening before), and told her now of my plans. I would attend classes the next day, and lead the noon meeting. Then Dink or Herby could drive me home in my car, depending on which one of them drove to campus.

I decided I would summarize the areas of the inerrancy debate, which I had covered in class and at the noon hour, so I would know where to go next in the noon study.

1. I had sought to introduce the present day inerrancy debate by doing the following:

    a. a summary of the old liberal view of the Bible
    b. a summary of the fundamentalist view of the Bible
    c. a summary of the neo-orthodox view of Karl Barth
    d. a summary of the errancy versus the inerrancy view

2. I had sought to show a distinction between errancy and inerrancy concerning the manner in which each view determines what kind of book the Bible is:

a. The errancy view uses the phenomena of the Bible.

b. The inerrancy view uses the testimony of the Bible concerning its own nature.

3. I had begun to answer some objections to inerrancy:

a. Inerrancy or verbal inspiration does not equal mechanical dictation.

b. The essence of Christianity is Christ not the Bible, but that does not negate the importance or the necessity of inerrancy of Scripture.

c. Rejecting inerrancy because we do not have the original manuscripts is not a valid argument but is a demand for total evidence rather than sufficient evidence, something (total evidence) we do not have for any other doctrinal conviction.

4. My next discussion would be to answer Dr. Avery's contention that Luther and Calvin did not believe in an inerrant Scripture.

As I was working on this fourth area, the motel phone rang.

"Is this Mr. Ira Pointer?" an unfamiliar voice asked.

"Yes it is! Who is this?" I insisted.

"This is Mack Turnover. I write for the *Seminary City Sentinel,* and wondered if you would have time to talk to me."

"What about?" I asked, having some suspicions he was stirring for a story on the Strawman.

"I understand that you have been involved in the battle on campus over the issue of inerrancy?" he offered.

"Why do you call the discussion of doctrine on a seminary campus a controversy? Is that not what young seminarians should be doing?" I quizzed. "And why do you call it the inerrancy battle? Could it not be called an errancy battle as well?"

"Look, kid!" he said condescendingly. "I'm going to get a story and write it regardless of whether you give me an interview or not. You can either cooperate and give me your view or you can let someone else influence my understanding of the whole affair. Make up your mind!"

I was tempted to say, "Well, kid, bring your crayons and coloring book, and I will draw some pictures for you of all the events." But I checked myself, and spoke more graciously.

'Look, all we are trying to do is learn theology---that's it!"

"Oh?" he exclaimed. "Do you call being shot at and beat up so you have to go to the hospital studying theology? Is it the study of theology for some idiot you call the Strawman to run around dressed up like a scarecrow?"

"Do you mean you want to publish something like that and spread it before the world?" I asked.

"Why not?" "That's my job!" he replied rather flippantly. "If we don't, someone else will. So how about it, kid? Will you see me?"

I didn't know anything about his religious views, but I tried to discourage him another way.

"Are you a Baptist?" I asked. "Are you an Evangelistic Baptist?"

"Yes, sir!" he replied rather emphatically.

"Are you a moderate or conservative?" I probed again.

"What difference does that make?" he returned.

"Well, if the Strawman turns out to be a moderate in his view of the Scripture (and it seems he may be since he is fighting against inerrancy so hard), it could be damaging to the moderate cause in the state and in our convention. Could you handle that?"

"I'll handle it! Don't worry about me!" he shot back, as if he had been through discussions of this nature before.

Because of his attitude and the uncertainty of his motives, I told him I would not grant an interview. I told him that I thought the whole issue would be better off left alone, as far as the media was concerned.

He then gave me one final squeeze.

"Okay, kid, but remember when you read the story, I gave you the first shot!"

I knew when he closed in that manner that he was not an honorable man, but I couldn't begin to understand what he meant with his last statement, until several weeks later.

I turned back to my preparation for the next day, as I told myself, "Kid, someone is stirring a lot of trouble, and it may very well get worse! Watch your step!"

28

What about Luther and the Bible...?

The next day I made it to school, and went to the cafeteria for the noon meeting. I summarized the material that Dr. Avery had given us in class concerning Luther.

1. Christ alone is without error.

2. Luther's faith was in the content of Scripture, though it has error, but nonetheless it reveals an inerrant Christ to us.

3. Luther did use words which seemed to indicate an inerrant Scripture, but he meant that the Bible was capable of revealing the inerrant Christ to us for the performance of God's work of His righteousness within us.

4. One must reinterpret any words which Luther spoke which seemed to indicate that he believed in an inerrant Scripture.

I told the men that I had real trouble with the last two ideas:

1. Luther did use words that seemed to indicate an inerrant Scripture.

2. But we must reinterpret these words to say he did not believe in an inerrant Scripture, but he meant that the Bible was errant but could reveal to us an inerrant Christ.

I asked them, if that is what Luther meant, why didn't he say it?

I then called their attention to a book devoted entirely to Luther's view of Scripture by a A. Skevington Wood. He gives one whole chapter to Luther's view of inspiration.[1] Some of the phrases of Luther in reference to Scripture are as follows:

...honour the Holy Spirit by believing his Words and accepting them as the divine truth...[2]

...inspiration extends to 'phraseology and diction'...[3]

...spoken by the Holy Spirit...[4]

...the prophets are those 'into whose mouth the Holy Spirit has given the words'...[5]

...the Scriptures have never erred...[6]

...the Scriptures cannot lie...[7]

...the perfectly clear, certain, sure words of God, which can never deceive us or allow to err...[8]

...prize a single tittle and letter more highly than the whole world...[9]

I next admitted that the phrase *Word of God* for Luther had a wide usage. He used it to refer to the Bible, the word of absolution, the word of promise, the gospel, and even the oral word of the sermon. The Word of God to him was something dynamic. But the Bible was the Word of God in a unique sense, as can be seen from the above-quoted references to it. The dynamic working of the Word of God in the other areas mentioned was dependent upon Scripture, which contained no deception---not even in one word.

I made several other points about Luther and the Bible. First, I noted, that his references to inspiration and inerrancy have been discarded by some because he gave evidence of being critical of Scripture, particularly some books and details. But one must remind himself, however, that Luther made no claim for the inerrancy of the manuscripts possessed in his day, but of the originals. His labors as a textual critic were attempts to determine the original text.

One must also remember Luther's historical situation. In many areas of the Christian faith he was seeking to sort out what was truly of God from what was only Roman Catholic tradition. If in the process he raised some jarring questions, one must remember the context from which he spoke and his ever clear adherence to an inerrant Scripture. One must not take statements that reflect Luther's struggles and interpret them to say that he denied inerrancy.

Finally, we must not read Luther in the light of the twentieth-century inerrancy debate, and then demand that he speak in our categories of thought. Categories of thought and definitions have changed because of the influx of neo-orthodoxy, which change has required a restatement and redefinition of the inerrancy position in order to provide more clarity now. Such clarity was not needed in Luther's day because the inerrancy of Scripture was not the issue.

Even so, Luther spoke with a clarity that comes through to us if we read him in his historical setting and consider all his statements regarding the nature of the Bible. He clearly subscribed to an inerrant Scripture.

After some brief discussion we closed. I was very tired and sensed I needed to go home. So I cornered Dink, and asked him if he would drive me home. He agreed, but I did not want to leave without telling Dr. Avery.

When he gave me permission to miss the evening class, he added something else.

"We are having our meeting with the Board on Monday to recommend Dr. William Post to serve on the faculty. Can you be there to answer any questions some might have, and to make any statement you wish concerning his qualification to serve or not to serve?"

"Do you expect some questions about his theology, or his view of the Bible?" I asked curiously.

"Yes," he replied, "With the national convention electing conservative presidents, all the new board members of recent date are conservatives. I am certain they will have some questions to ask."

"You can't tell them his views?" I asked, trying not to let my weariness in body or my weariness of his ride-the-fence attitude show.

"I could, but you can do it better!" he affirmed.

I told him I would have to wait and see how I felt, but that I would do my best to attend the meeting. I mentioned I would have to stay in Seminary City in the motel again, and though I was not hinting for it, he said the seminary would pick up the tab.

I slept all the way home, having no idea what I would have to face that next Monday!

[1]A. Skevington Wood, *Captive to the Word: Martin Luther: Doctor of Sacred Scripture* (Grand Rapids: Eerdmans, 1969), pp. 139-48.

[2]Martin Luther, *Luther's Works*, ed. Jaroslav J. Pelikan and Helmut T. Lehmann, 55 vols. (Philadelphia and St. Louis, 1955-), 22:10. (Also in Wood, pp. 141-142.)

[3]Luther, *Works*, 22:119. (Also in Wood, p. 143.)

[4]Martin Luther, *D. Martin Luthers samtliche Schriften*, ed. Johann Georg Walch, 24 vols. Revised. (St. Louis, 1890-1910), 3:1895. (Also in Wood, p. 141).

[5]Martin Luther, D. *Martin Luthers Werke, kritische Gesamtausgabe*, ed. J. F. K. Knaake et al, 57 vols. (Weimer, 1883-), 3:172. (Also in Wood, p. 142)

[6]Luther, *Works*, 32:11. (Also in Wood, p. 144.)

[7]Luther, *Works*, 27:258. (Also in Wood, p. 144.)

[8]Luther, *Works*, 47:308. (Also in Wood, p. 145.)

[9]Luther, *Works*, 37:308. (Also in Wood, p. 145.)

29

Who Could Imagine Me at a Seminary Board Meeting...?

I certainly possessed some mixed emotions as I made the trip to Seminary City on Monday for an afternoon meeting of the board. Somehow I was not certain of all the motives behind my invitation, anymore that I had been of my inclusion in the student meeting with Dr. Post. I kept wondering if all the kindness being shown towards me was to convince someone that the seminary was seeking to be open to some conservative thinking.

The meeting of the board started about 2:00 P.M., but they said they would not call me until that certain point of business concerning Dr. Post came up, which would be no earlier than 4:00 P.M. It wasn't until 4:30 that I was called into the meeting room.

It was an expansive and elegant room, with an individual seat and desk for each board member, something like you might see in pictures of state legislative bodies. I sat down in a single chair off to the side, as I was instructed. The chairman of the board, someone I had never met, called for the next order of business.

Whichever committee was responsible for such things (I think maybe it was the Academic Committee), made the recommendation that the school hire Dr. William Post to serve in the New Testament Department on the faculty. As in most business meetings, someone made the motion, another seconded it, and the floor was opened for discussion.

It seemed no one was going to say anything or ask any questions, until a brother in the back rose to speak.

"I want to know one thing. Does he believe the Bible is the inspired Word of God?"

I wasn't sure who he was, but from my recent experience I noted that if he was a conservative wanting a defining answer, he hadn't asked the question clearly enough. The chairman of the committee finally sought to answer the question.

"I would hope that this board has such a trust in the present administration and faculty here that you would know we would not recommend a man if he denied the authority and inspiration of Scripture. So to answer your question, Dr. Post does believe the Bible is the inspired Word of God!"

The conservative questioner, whoever he was, was not finished. Maybe he had faced previously these word games that some moderates played in theology, especially concerning the doctrine of the nature of Scripture.

Dr. Avery spoke up, and I may have found out why he wanted me to be present.

"Mr. Ira Pointer, one of our students, is with us today, and he might help us here. He asked Dr. Post that very question in an interview session. Mr. Pointer, perhaps you can answer the question. What does Dr. Post believe about the Bible?"

He then invited me to come to the podium to speak, in case there were questions. As I stood to my feet and walked to the front of the room, I pondered my impossible situation. I wasn't sure who made up this board, but it probably had doctors, lawyers, business men, other professionals and some preachers who were conservatives, and some who were moderates. How could I possibly in two or three minutes enlighten them concerning the battle for the Bible which was going on in our seminary and school? I concluded that it was too much to expect them to understand the intricate theology behind it, and I knew most of them were probably carry-overs from the past moderate regime, which indicated where they stood. So what could I say?

"I asked Dr. Post the following question!" I began. "What is your position on the nature of Scripture?" His answer was, "I believe the Bible to be the Word of God."

"I was not satisfied with that answer, so I asked Dr. Post to elaborate further on my question, because many, even Karl Barth, could answer as he had.

"He replied something like this: 'The Bible is our record of the revelation of God. It is the Word about God, it is the Word from God, it is the Word to reveal God, it is the Word to fulfill the purpose of God, and it is the Word whereby we encounter the truth of God.'" I was glad I had kept careful notes of our encounter.

I continued.

"I could see as he spoke this second time to answer my question, that he was upset with me for probing further into his beliefs. But I spoke to him again to seek to get a direct and clear answer.

"I told him he had given me a Barthian view of Scripture, and then I asked him very directly, 'Is the Bible inspired in the sense that it is the infallible and inerrant Word of God in its original manuscripts? Or to put it another way, would you agree with the statement that God has revealed himself in history, and that revelation has been recorded in a verbal and plenarily inspired inerrant and infallible Bible in its original manuscripts?'

"He then became abusive in language, and laughed, and said my questions were ignorant and shallow. He berated me for asking such questions of him, in light of his education and scholarship, and in light of the fact I was only a freshman in the seminary. He compared me to the men who troubled Job, and said the denomination would be better off without the likes of me. He said if there were more students like me at the school, he was not sure he would want to teach here."

I wasn't sure when to quit in trying to communicate these matters to the board. I decided I would add a couple of more points as conclusions.

"I think it is clear from this episode what Dr. Post believes about the Bible, and that if he is added to the faculty, there will be a great turmoil on campus over this doctrine of the nature of Scripture. I do not recommend that he be hired to serve on the faculty!"

The place erupted, with board members speaking without being recognized. The brother who had asked the question stated, "That settles it for me. How can we hire a liberal like that?"

One moderate blurted out, "The student's original question is ridiculous! We don't even have the original manuscripts!"

Another moderate voiced, "All of this arguing in the denomination has nothing to do with theology. Its all politics as a bunch of conservatives are trying to take over the denomination!"

When he spoke, I noticed he was the man who had been the moderator at the ordination service that had helped propel me into this quest.

Finally, the Chairman gaveled the gathering to order with some rebuke in his voice.

"Men, men! Settle down. Now we are going to deal with this in a sane and gentlemanly manner!"

He then turned to Dr. Avery, and asked him what he thought was best, in light of the situation in the denomination, in light of the controversy on campus already, and now in light of the upheaval of this board. I hoped I would find out now his true heart, but then I was reminded that he might do only that which was best for his career and future relationship to the denomination.

"Mr. Pointer has given you an accurate picture of his encounter with Dr. Post. He was very kind and humble in asking his questions, but Dr. Post became abusive and belittling and condescending in his reaction. I recommend that we look for another candidate, and that we do not hire Dr. Post. I know that every other person on every other committee was in favor of Dr. Post, but we have seen in the last few weeks a division over these matters on campus, and now we have seen it in this board. Surely we can find someone who will be more acceptable to all of us."

When the board voted, it was close, but nonetheless, Dr. Post was rejected, and now the door was open for another candidate to be pursued. But I had to wonder, what kind of a candidate would satisfy both sides of the controversy?

I gave a sigh of relief as I headed home! I had to come up the next day, but I wanted nothing to do with anybody's bed but my own---no motel, but especially no hospital bed.

I didn't' realize then, but the battle was about to be escalated even higher in the following days!

30

Are You Sure You Really Know Who the Strawman Is...?

It was a boring trip back to the seminary on Tuesday morning. Not even the usual chatter of Dink, or the over-exuberance of Herby could perk me up. Dink was praising the Lord over the previous evening's events, as he had been witnessing in the prison. Herby was telling of the soul he had led to Christ yesterday afternoon. I was the only one dragging that morning, but I did look forward eagerly to the noon meeting. I was going to give an answer to the claim that John Calvin did not believe in the inerrancy of Scripture.

When we parked on the campus, I found someone waiting for me. It was Mack Turnover of the *Seminary City Sentinel*. He was young, and in his late twenties, and it was obvious that he hadn't learned anything about making friends and influencing people as he addressed me.

"Hey, kid, come over here!" he said as he motioned to me when I stepped out of the car.

I thought Dink was going to come unglued over his cockiness.

"Whose ya talkin to der, Buster?" Dink asked.

"I'm talking to Pointer there. What's it to you, dumbbell!" he countered with greater arrogance.

If I hadn't caught his arm, there's no telling what Dink might have done to him.

"Its okay, Dink. I'll take care of him. He's from the press---a newspaper man." I noted.

"Well, dat Bozo needs a lesson. He ain't gonna talk ta my preacha dat way. Dis here's Pastuh Pointer ta youse, an if youse mistreats him, I'll give ya a deadline ya won't be able ta meet!"

"Well, what do you want, Turnover?" I asked with some disdain in my voice.

"That was quite a meeting you guys had yesterday in the board room, wasn't it?"

"What went on in there is none of your business, unless the president of the seminary or the chairman of the board chooses to let you in on the events which took place," I stated emphatically.

"Yeah, well, answer me this one," he said with a smart-aleck laugh. "When are you going to apply for the job? You know all about theology---enough to shoot down a promising candidate for a faculty opening."

"Are you trying to tell me that you know what went on at that meeting?" I inquired.

"Yep, I got a voice tape of everything! I want to give you one last chance to tell me your side of the story before I write it. How about it, kid?"

I thought to myself, "What a creep! He obviously has some knowledge of the meeting, but does he have a tape? He wouldn't dare admit that publicly. He would simply say that a newsman has the right to guard his sources."

I finally replied to him, "Not in a thousand years! I don't like you, your attitude, or your media manner. Print what you want! We will leave it in the Lord's hands!"

"You mean you don't mind taking the blame for a greater explosion over this thing than has come already? Look, kid, this could ruin your ministerial career. I understand you're a pretty smart and brainy kind of guy, and it seems to me you might want to teach in a college or seminary some day. Can you imagine having this on your record for the rest of your life? Yep, I'll blow you, the Strawman, the school, the president, and everything clear out of the water with my article. And it will be from a moderate viewpoint---unless you cooperate."

I didn't appreciate any of his threats, but especially I felt concern for Dr. Avery, whatever his motives. He seemed to be making some kind of allowance and opening for the conservative viewpoint---something you couldn't say about many of the moderates who had been in control.

"Get lost, Turnover!" I firmly commanded. "I learned a long time ago that God fights my battles, just as long as I am doing His will. But I sure would be worried, if I were in your shoes, and pulled off what you are threatening. You talk about ruining my future, but just remember that God at times turns the gun intended for another back on the perpetrator of the crime. Have you ever heard of Haman in the Bible? I may be the one who has to witness you picking up the pieces of your life and career!"

With that I left him still threatening me.

"Just watch the papers for my article!"

Somehow my mind wasn't on Calvin as I hurried for the noon meeting! But then I was encouraged as I remembered he had suffered many threats in his life and ministry also.

31

What about Calvin's View of the Bible...?

I began my noon presentation by summarizing Dr. Avery's convictions about Calvin's view of the Scriptures.

1. All men have an innate knowledge of God which is suppressed by their sin.

2. Therefore, God has given man a better way of knowledge, and that is the revelation of Scripture.

3. We must be careful not to elevate the Scripture above Christ.

4. The primary purpose of Scripture is to reveal Christ in a saving way, and we must not demand any kind of inerrancy in Scripture in order for it to be able reveal Christ to us.

I then made the following statement:

As it was for Luther, so it is with Calvin---men jump to the conclusion that he could not believe in an inerrant Scripture, but they do so without solid fact or argument. The truth of the matter is that Calvin speaks of such an inerrant text in terms that very clearly indicate a belief in inerrancy.

I then gave some quotations from Calvin:

But since no daily responses are given from heaven, and the Scriptures are the only records in which God has been pleased to consign his truth to perpetual remembrance, the full authority which they ought to possess with the faithful is not recognized, unless they are believed to have come from heaven, as directly as if God had been heard giving utterance to them.[1]

Hence, the highest proof of Scripture is uniformly taken from the character of him whose word it is.[2]

Nay, words uniformly said by the prophets to have been spoken by the Lord of Hosts, are by Christ and his apostles ascribed to the Holy Spirit. Hence it follows that the Spirit is the true Jehovah, who dictated the prophecies.[3]

Although, as I have observed, there is this difference between the apostles and their successors, they were sure and authentic amanuenses of the Holy Spirit; and, therefore, their writings are to be regarded as the oracles of God, whereas others have no other office than to teach what is delivered and sealed in the holy Scriptures.[4]

I concluded by noting there are more arguments in the debate on both sides, but this should be sufficient to introduce the student to the main issues of the problem. Some discussion followed, but no opposition arose over the matter. Thus we dismissed and hurried to our early afternoon class.

After this class, Dink called me aside and wanted to know if we could go to Handy Andy's Hamburgers. He wanted to share something with me that he had just learned. Herby said he needed to study, so we took off.

When seated at Handy's with a cool refreshing milk shake, he opened, with eyes bigger than doughnuts.

"I knows who da Strawman is!" he whispered.

"Who? And don't forget the evidence!" I reminded.

"Da Strawman is dat Mack Turnover guy from da newspaper! Before class this morning, while youse guys was jawin, I snuck up on his car and looked in da window. Guess what! I saw da Strawman disguise sticken out from under some papers in the back. He'd tried to cover it up, but it was sticken out just enough for me ta see what it was!"

"How much of it was showing from under the papers?" I asked.

"Bout a foot---an it was da Strawman suit---believe me ---I'd know it anywhere."

"Where's his car now?" I asked eagerly.

"Its gone! He took off just after he needled ya. But we could find his house, an I could break in da car---dat sure would prove it was him!" he offered, ready to use his trade from the past for the Lord's glory.

"Well, Dink, we can't do that. We have to work within the law. It may sound unfair to the law-abiding citizen sometimes, when criminals play by no rules, and we are bound by the law, but that is the way it has to be according to the Book! We can't be arguing for the inerrancy of Scripture, and then turn around and ignore it or misinterpret it in a way just so it will benefit us. The law is the law and we must follow it!"

"Well is der anyting dat says ya can't help da law?" he muttered. "If not, I'se got sumptin in mind!"

"Is it legal?" I pressed him.

"Yep, its sumptin kinda like we used once in da gang ta catch some guy we knew who had double-crossed us, but we couldn't prove it. Boy did we get him."

"Dink, I think you'd better tell me about this! I'd need to know what's coming and if its really legal." I insisted.

"Okay, Preacha, but I'll guarantee ya right now that its gonna please ya. It's called a sting!"

"But what if he's not the Strawman?" I asked

"If he's not, it ain't gonna hurt him. If he is, it'll nail him?" Dink said gleefully, enjoying this opportunity to use his old knowledge and experience for the Lord---within the law---I hoped!!!

---

1.   John Calvin, *The Institutes of Christian Religion,* trans. Henry Beveridge, 2 vols. (Grand Rapids: Eerdmans, 1964), 1:68.

2.   Ibid., 1:71.

3.   Ibid., 1:23.

4.   Ibid., 2:395.

32

How Could a Man Tell Such Lies...?

Wednesday was a rather common day (praise the Lord), but not Thursday morning. When I picked Dink up to head for school, he asked, "Well, have ya seen it yet?"

"Seen what?" I asked?

"Mack Turnover's article is in da morning papers---both da *Seminary City Sentinel* and den our local paper, da *Collegetown Globe*. You'se gonna be shocked, Preacha!" he declared as he handed me a copy.

I pulled over to the side of the road to read it, and was flabbergasted even at the headline: DENOMINATIONAL SEMINARY IS EXPLODED IN CONTROVERSY BY YOUNG STUDENT-PASTOR.

The article took its start from the rejection of the candidacy of Dr. Post as a faculty member, and described the board meeting as a "knock-down, drag-out" affair spurred by the insistent intrusion of a young trouble-maker named Ira Pointer. I had insisted, the article said, on being allowed to speak to the board, and because of my threats to take the whole matter public to a higher level to stir the denominational controversy further, the president, Dr. Avery, had allowed me to speak. When I spoke, I did not do as I had agreed, but exploded the whole meeting by insisting that they not hire Dr. Post because he was not a "fighting fundamentalist" like I was.

Mack, in his biased article so full of lies, went on to blame me for the Strawman incident on campus. He said I had been leading a noon study which promoted a view of the Bible known as "inerrancy," which is equal to mechanical dictation. This is an old-fashioned, narrow-minded, legalistic view of the Bible, and it was being used by a group of conservatives to grab power in the denomination. The battle is not really theological, he said, (and if theological views are brought in, it is only to deceive). The real battle is a struggle to take over a denomination, which for years has been free of such controversy, until the rise of these narrow men.

Mack noted that my presence on the campus in just a few months had led to students being shot at and beaten so badly they had to be taken to the hospital (he failed to tell the reading audience that I was the one fired on and beaten, and his use of the plural "they" led to the conclusion that there were many instances and not just one). And though he did not say so, he left the impression that the Strawman was a device of the "fundamentalists" to stir the controversy.

He also claimed that I had taken over a theology class, by stirring up the other students, to the extent the regular teacher had to be removed, and the president of the school had to be brought in to keep peace in the class. Also, part of the negotiations for peace in the class, led by Mr. Pointer, was that he be allowed to teach several sessions on his unscholarly view of the Bible.

Mack's final shot was a brief excursion into my history. He had obtained some information about the incidents at First Baptist Church of Collegetown while I was there as pastor,[1] and had twisted them also to show I was a divisive person and pastor. He also implied that I was the reason my successor at First Baptist Church, Durwood Girvin, alias James Seavers (and Samuel Seavers' brother) had his problems at the church, Finally, this was the reason, he said, that I carried a supposed-animosity towards Samuel Seavers, the teacher in the class where I had created the explosion to get him removed from teaching.

In closing he urged the seminary board to investigate all of these matters, and deal with the leader of these negative, trouble-making students, as well as his followers. He also urged the denomination, by whatever means they governed their seminaries, to take some action against me, and set up some rules whereby nothing of this kind could happen again.

"Well, that settles it!" I informed Dink. "The sting is on ---tell me about it in full detail!"

33

Do You Know You're under the Big Boss's Wrath...?

As we drove to school that Thursday, Dink outlined for me his proposed "sting" for Mack Turnover. It was brilliant in many respects, but especially in the fact it broke no law and was even going to give Mr. Turnover a spiritual lesson. We decided we would put it into effect on Friday evening of this week.

Thus on that specified Friday, we gathered at a remote place in Collegetown to begin the sting. We felt like members of the "Mission Impossible" gang. We all came dressed gangster style---black suit, dark shirt, and white necktie, with a black hat (except for me as I had a chauffeur's cap) and we all had sunglasses to wear to keep from being recognized. I wondered how those sunglasses would work in the dark, but I would soon find out. It was clear that no one was going to be able to recognize us this night.

Dink came, as planned, with a black limousine he had borrowed from some old pals. The group included Dink and I, and our local policeman friend and church member, Troy Medford, and, of course, Herby. The plan had been explained to everyone, and they were ready to fulfill their part. We were prepared to spend all night, if necessary, to carry out our mission.

Dink called Mack's house, hoping he was home, and we smiled and rejoiced silently, when Dink began to speak to him in a husky voice.

"Is dis Mr. Mack Turnover? Well, listen to me, Jack! I'se gots a story for ya, if youse wants it."

We were banking on Mack not being able to resist the thought of a story. And sure enough, it was clear he was taking the bait, as we listened carefully to one side of the conversation.

"Look, Jack, I'll tell ya what da story's all about, if ya wanna meet wid us. Be out in front of yur house tonight at 11:00 and we'll pick ya up. But dis has got ta be strictly confidential. Got it? See ya den, Jack!"

When Dink hung up, we shook our fists into the air and rejoiced. The sting had begun. We had not lied to him--- we did have a story for him---one he might not like, but a story nevertheless, and one he would never forget.

We left Collegetown about 8:00 P.M. and drove inconspicuously to Seminary City. We tooled slowly past Mack's house, and sure enough, there he was waiting out front. I was driving, thinking that would be the most prudent manner for me to participate without being recognized. I pulled up to the curb, and Dink got out in the dark, and the conversation began.

"Get in, Jack!" I heard him say in his husky gangster voice. "We don't want nobody ta see us."

Mack got in, though I am sure he was a little apprehensive about our procedure, and I don't blame him. The limousine was dimly and briefly lit when the doors were open---just enough for him to see that there were three men staring him down, plus a chauffeur. It must have been a frightening and foreboding situation, but it seems, his newspaper nose led him on.

I pulled out into the street, made my way to the nearest interstate highway, thinking a black limousine would be least conspicuous there than on the streets of Seminary City. I drove out away from town, as Dink confronted Mack in the darkness, as the tinted windows kept out even the lights of the passing cars and trucks.

"Da Big Boss sent us ta talk ta ya. It seems dat youse under His wrath," Dink declared, referring to the Lord.

"The Big Boss? Who...,uh...., who, uh, is..., is that?" he asked with some fear.

"The Biggest Boss anywhere. Ya can't get no higher dan Him! An youse are under His wrath!" Dink said again. I thought of Romans 1:18.

"Uh..., under his wrath? Uh..., uh..., for what?" he asked with clear evidence he felt the intimidation.

"For your wrong-doins and breakin of da law. Da Big Boss don't take it lightly when youse breaks His law."

Mack continued to be puzzled as he asked, "But what wrong-doings? What laws have I broken? I'm just a newspaper writer trying to make a living," he pled.

"It seems youse been messin wid one of da Big Boss's boys---writin untruthful tings bout him and his work."

"No, no, that's not possible. I don't even know any of the Big Boss's boys. I don't even know the Big Boss. I never write about Him, or His guys, or His work. You must have me mixed up with someone else!" he stated pleadingly.

"Youse don't know a Mr. Ira Pointer, and youse never wrote dat article published dis week so full of lies about Mr. Pointer?" Dink said confrontingly.

"Do you mean to say, uh, that Mr. Pointer is one of the Big Boss's boys?" he asked trying to appear innocent.

"Yep, an you might be interested to know dat Mr. Pointer talks to da Big Boss every day---sometimes two or tree times a day---even more!"

"Wow---I didn't know that. I..., I..., thought he was just some little preacher or pastor! I had no idea he had any connections to the Big Boss!" he declared apologetically.

"What's more, Mr. Pointer's got a very special and unique relationship wid the Big Boss's Son. He talks ta Him two or tree time a day too, or more! Dey is real close ---I mean real close."

It was clear that Mack was getting scared and uncertain about where this interview might end. He still had not realized that Dink was talking about God, and His Son Jesus Christ, and my relationship to Them.

"Hey, man, I'm sorry if I've offended the Big Boss. Wha.., what can I do to make it up. Anything---just tell me and I will do it."

"Well, youse knows, don't ya, dat da Big Boss could rub youse out any second he wants to? Even now...!" Dink said pressing him.

"Oh, yes! I suppose that's true too!" he stated reflectively.

"Suppose? Der's no supposin bout it. And youse knows dat da Big Boss knows everyting!---I mean everyting!" Dink said applying the vise.

"Everything?" he asked with deepening shock.

"Yep, everyting. He knows that youse are da Strawman," speaking truthfully, but yet fishing for further information for us. "And He knows dat youse gotta helper in dat affair---an He knows who he is!"

I heard a deep gulp from Mack.

"And da Big Boss knows bout da shootin an da attack on His boy, Mr. Pointer, an bout da weasel methods and lies ya wrote in dat dirtbag article in dat sleazy ting youse calls a newspaper. An He knows bout your proud and puffed up attitude towards Mr. Pointer, an da disrespectful words towards him too. If ders one ting da Big Boss don't put up wid, its insultin one of His chosen boys."

I found myself amazed at the theology coming out in Dink's interview---sin, sorrow for sin, repentance, even election, no less.

"Now," Dink continued, "Whaddaya tink da Big Boss ought ta do widda guy like you?"

"Uh, I guess I deserve the worst, uh, kind of punishment. But please, doesn't the Big Boss give people second chances?" he stated as he was begging for mercy now. "Doesn't he have any forgiveness in his heart. Surely he doesn't blow people away if they are willing to make things right with him."

I was amazed that men would be so fearful of men, and so willing, it seems, to make things right with men, but still treat God with such arrogance and disdain in light of Who He is and what He can do in comparison to men.

"Well, youse got dat right." Dink answered. "He's a pretty gracious person when men are really sincere in makin tings right."

"Please, what does he want me to do to make things right! I'll do anything---anything---I mean anything he asks!" he begged again.

"Well here is what da Big Boss asks ya ta do!" Dink declared with a delight in his voice. And then he gave him a list of necessary items:

1. Write a second article about Mr. Pointer, telling the truth, the full truth and nothing but the truth. We

would have to approve it for the Big Boss before it went to print. But then it has to be printed.

2. Identify his accomplice in the Strawman affair, and make clear the part each one of them had in the unfolding of all of those events.

3. Confess to the police his part in the Strawman affair by writing a confession to those crimes, stating with full accuracy who was involved in each part, and clearly acknowledging his crimes in those events. We would approve it in behalf of the Big Boss, and then he would take it to the police, and be willing to suffer all the legal consequences which might follow---even time in jail, if necessary.

4. Keep strictly confidential the contact he has had or would have with us tonight or in the days to come The police were not to know about us---no one--- that means no one was to know of us. It must be as if we never existed to other people. He was not to lie, but if he kept quiet about us, then no one would ever know what led him to these decisions.

When Dink handed these stipulations to him, Mack eagerly agreed with all of them. He would do exactly as we had asked, so he said. Knowing our "interview" with Mack was coming to an end, I turned into a deserted area a few blocks from his house. I turned the lights off as Dink added the final touch.

"Now we know dat ya might be tempted to pull a double-cross on us. But just remember dose in da past who tried a double-cross on da Big Boss. One ended up hanging himself [I recognized that one as Judas], one was stoned to death along wid his family [I recognized this one as Achan], and anudder spent the rest of his life exiled with insanity [I recognized this one as Pilate]."

Dink then opened the door for Mack to get out. As he exited, it was an eerie near-darkness which robbed him of a full view of anyone of us.

"How can I get in touch with you guys?" he asked with some hesitancy.

"Don't worry!" Dink replied. "We'll be in touch which youse. Just have dat material ready in a few days!"

Then the doors closed, and the tinted glass swallowing us became our protection. Plus, I backed out so he could not get our license number.

34

Will You Take Sunday Dinner with Us...?

By the time we arrived home Saturday morning, it was almost 5:00 A.M. I toppled into bed, slept a few hours, only to be awakened by the phone. Guess who was calling!

"Pastor Pointer? This is Mack Turnover."

I was still tired, but I didn't dare show it on the phone. I noticed that he didn't address me as "kid."

"I have done you a great injustice, and I want to apologize!" he offered.

I didn't say anything, but waited for him to go on.

"Are you still there?"

"Yes, I am here. You can continue!"

"Well, I want to apologize for that sleazy article I wrote, but even more than that, I need to apologize for my attitude towards you---my pride, my manipulation of events to get a story, my involving others in my wrong-doing---well, can you forgive me for all of that?"

"Yes, I suppose, if your apology is sincere!" I replied, testing him.

"Oh, its sincere---and you can tell anyone who might ask you that I am very sincere!" he declared emphatically, perhaps hoping I would pass the word on to the Big Boss.

"But how can I know you are sincere?" I asked, leading him to share with me his intent or lack of intent to carry out our stipulations.

"Yes, yes, I do need to prove my sincerity, and I will tell you how. I am writing a second article, and will tell the truth, the whole truth and nothing but the truth. And I know you may not think I am trustworthy, but I would really like to interview you just to be sure I get the truth."

I was rejoicing to hear this, but needed to test him again to be sure he was serious.

"How do I know that this is not just another one of your manipulative schemes to get an interview so you can write a follow-up article to your last one?" I asked.

"Well, I know I don't deserve to be trusted, but, please, you've got to believe me this one time. Please, please, it could be a matter of life or death for me. Please!"

"I'll tell you what!" I offered. "Let's meet so I can see you face to face. Then if there's more you need to tell me to convince me, I will listen. Then I will make a decision on your request."

"When can we meet! It needs to be soon! I need to get these things finished in just a few day!" he spoke forcefully, but with humility.

"How about tomorrow?" I asked.

"Tomorrow? Sunday?" he countered.

"Yes, you come to our morning services at 10:45 A.M., and then come to dinner to meet my wife and family, and we can spend the afternoon going over these matters, as you wish!" I offered.

"Would you? Would you really?" he marveled out-loud, in seeming unbelief. "After all I've done and said against you, you would have me in your home?"

"Yes, that's the way of Christ! And if yours is a sincere repentance, I wish to help you straighten things out, not only with me, but with God also."

I had wanted an opportunity to preach the gospel to him and now it seemed I was going to get it.

He agreed, and we began making preparations for his visit, which included, among other things, the preparation of our people for the attendance at our services of the man who had just lambasted their pastor maliciously and falsely. In fact, my wife had been doing little more than manning the phone since the article ran in the paper. So we set in motion our prayer line which shared the information that Mack Turnover was coming to our church, and the need to show him love and grace.

Wouldn't it be great and just like the Lord to open his heart to Christ through all of this mess?

35

What Happened to Change Your Life...?

Mack was present at the Sunday morning worship service, and I gave the message a strong evangelistic thrust, as I spoke on God's holiness and wrath against sinners, yet His mercy to forgive through His Son when there was sincere repentance of sin and faith in Christ. Our people welcomed him too.

After dinner, which went well also, when Ira, Jr. had been put down for a nap, Terry and I and Mack sat down in the living room, and he began to share with us all he had done against me. The following matters came to light, as the puzzle I had wrestled with for those weeks emerged with clarity.

He admitted that he was the Strawman. He was the one who had appeared in the school cafeteria the first time. He was the one who had twisted the windshield wipers of Herby's car. He was the one who had scratched a message on the hood of my car. He was the one who had shot at us. He was the one who had hit me with the tire iron in the dark. He was the one who had made all the phone calls, except one.

He also confessed that he had hid a tape recorder in the seminary board room, and he had started it by remote control when he saw me enter for my moments with the board. He admitted that he also had written the article for the newspaper in a biased fashion and gotten involved in the whole situation due to the urging of someone else, as he had no real convictions about who was right and who was wrong in the battle over the Bible. All he wanted was a story.

I then offered a question.

"Who is the one who got you involved in this matter, and is that the same one who made the other phone call?"

"The other party is Samuel Seavers," he continued. "He contacted me just after he was relieved of his teaching duties in regards to that class. He said there was a story brewing on the campus between two theological viewpoints, and wanted to know if I was interested in following it. He appeared to be angry that he had bombed in the classroom, and wanted to get even with you, as he saw you to be the catalyst."

"Was he involved in the creation of the Strawman, and all those pranks growing out of that?" I asked.

"No, he just wanted me to get a story. I created all the rest, and I take responsibility for it. He did call you that one time, and I really don't know why. Maybe he just got caught up in it all, and couldn't contain himself."

"Then your whole motive was neither the theological issue nor a personal action against me, but the desire for a story for yourself, and the hope you could escalate the story into a major one by some strange accompanying events? Is that right?" I asked, just to be sure.

"That's correct! And I am sorry!" he stated again.

"But what happened to turn you around so quickly?" I asked, testing him once again.

"Well, I had a life-changing experience the other night that I am not free to discuss. I have to do what I am doing today, and I will continue to pursue the resolving of this matter whatever the cost."

"Life-changing experience?" I queried. "That sounds like a religious experience!"

"I don't know all the whys and wherefores myself as I look over this thing, nor do I know where it will end. Maybe the Lord is speaking to me about something! Maybe I do need what you preached about this morning! Maybe I am a sinner who is under the wrath of God. I've got a lot to think about in the next few days, including this."

He then interviewed me, as I told him I truly thought I could trust him. We went through the whole past few weeks, and all the events, and the motives which had driven me. I assured him I had sought to stand for the truth in a loving and yet godly manner without compromise. I also assured him I have found out in my few years in ministry, that even when you stand for the truth with the right attitude, that does not mean every one will love you, accept you, or attribute to you the real motives of your heart. You will be misunderstood, misrepresented, maligned, and falsely accused time and again. But you can only keep reassessing your heart to be sure it is right with God, and continue to follow the way of truth and righteousness regardless of how men treat you or what they say about you.

When we had finished Mack thanked me, and asked if we could stay in touch.

"I may be going away in a few days to a very unpleasant place, and it may be necessary for me to try to get all of this straightened out. I would like to have you as a friend and counselor through this ordeal, if I could."

I agreed to do anything I could at any time, and urged him to feel free to call upon me. He then apologized to Terry for any grief he had brought to her also.

36

Were Those Angels in That Limousine...?

The next day, a Monday, Dink called Mack and made arrangements anonymously to pick up his corrected newspaper article and his confession. When we had read them and made a few suggestions for changes for the sake of clarity, he turned in his article to his editor with a copy of his confession, and a plea to publish the new article with an apology to the newspaper and to me. He then went to the police station, turned himself in, and threw himself on the mercy of the court. Samuel Seavers was arrested also, and charges were brought against him.

We (Herby and Dink and I) visited them both often, but received little response from Seavers. He seemed to remain bitter over the whole turn of events.

One day when we went in to visit Mack, he smiled and say, "Guys, I did it! I came to Christ by faith and repentance of my sins."

We all cried and praised God together for awhile.

Then he said, "This whole ordeal has been worth it all, and any time I spend in jail will be a joyful time, as I know I am in His will, and I will now serve Him for the rest of my life."

Then he made a request.

"Can I tell you guys something?---something you may not believe? I think this was all brought about by a strange visit from some angels. They didn't look like angels, and they didn't talk like angels, but they seem to be angels to me now as I think back on it. But, boy, no one would have ever taken them to be angels by their looks."

Then he turned to Herby and said, "And you, brother, do you remember all the times you cornered me on campus and witnessed to me about the wrath of God and the love of God, and the grace of God to forgive sinners if we repent and believe? Boy, I hated you for that. But you know, as I have searched and thought about it, you talked just like those angels---about the wrath of a Big Boss, and the love of the Big Boss, and the forgiveness of the Big Boss, and so on. I thought they were talking about some earthly Big Boss. Pastor Ira, do you think they could have been talking about God?"

I was trying to think of something to say when he started talking again.

"And, Brother Ira, they said that you knew the Big Boss, and you knew his son, and you talked to them many times during the day. Could they have been talking about your relationship to God through Christ?"

I was scraping my brain again, when he took the ball.

"You know, there was so much similarity between the witness Herby gave me, and the message these angels gave me (though I didn't understand it that way at first), that I have come to the conclusion Herby and those angels were both sharing the gospel with me. Then I realized that I was so fearful of men, when I should have been fearful of God. And it was then I knew I needed to be saved."

"Brother Ira, do you think those men could have been angels?"

I explained, "The word angel means messenger---they do seem to have been messengers from God!"

He still wouldn't quit.

"But were they heavenly beings sent from God to this earth for that mission of showing me my need of Christ?"

I saw we needed to tell him the truth about this matter. So I said, "Don't you think the chauffeur was the best looking of those guys? And did you ever see anyone handle a limousine like he did?"

Dink jumped in next.

"Nah, da best guy was da leaduh. He was da one leadin ya right down da path of salvation."

Herby jumped in.

"But the best looking one was the short one. He didn't say anything, but he sure was convincing in his silence that he was a representative of the Big Boss."

It was something to watch Mack's face. His ears perked up and he listened intently. Confusion and a puzzled look flooded his expression. And then there came a big smile.

"How did you guys know these angels were in a limousine? You guys were the angels!!?? Oh, I don't believe it!" he stated, believing it nonetheless.

I wondered how he would react, knowing this event had sent him to jail.

"I just want to say, 'Thanks guys!' What an unusual way to witness in an unusual situation, and God used it! You guys will be my friends forever!"

"Yes, all through eternity!" I marveled.

"Hey der Mack! Ya know, youse a lot like me. Ya ain't such a bad guy now dat da Lord saved ya!" chided Dink.

"I'll say this!" declared Mack in the spirit of our jest. "I won't ever call you a dumbbell again, Dink, because you've got smarts like few guys I've seen (even though you talk funny). And, Herby, I'll never laugh at you again because you witness to everything that moves, and some things that don't. God used your witness to me. And Pastor Ira, I'll never call you 'kid' again, because you're one of the most mature young guys for your age that I have ever met. And I will guarantee you all that I will never be a Strawman again---I'm a Bible man all the way."

We had a time of prayer and parted with tears flowing down our cheeks and praises rising to heaven---the sting had stung the devil, and robbed him of one of his most aggressive servants! What could be better than that?

37

Have We Counted the Cost of Theological Battle...?

In the next few days I summarized again in my notes the areas of the inerrancy debate which we had covered. The summary was as follows:

1. I had sought to introduce the present day inerrancy debate by doing the following:

   a. a summary of the old liberal view of the Bible
   b. a summary of the fundamentalist view of the Bible
   c. a summary of the neo-orthodox view of Karl Barth
   d. a summary of the errancy versus the inerrancy view

2. I had sought to show a distinction between errancy and inerrancy concerning their method of the determination of the nature of the Bible:

   a. The errancy view uses the phenomena of the Bible.

   b. The inerrancy view uses the testimony or the Bible concerning its own nature.

3. I had begun to answer some objections to inerrancy:

    a.   Inerrancy or verbal inspiration does not equal mechanical dictation.

    b.   The essence of Christianity is Christ not the Bible, but that does not negate the importance or the necessity of inerrancy of Scripture.

    c.   Rejecting inerrancy because we do not have the original manuscripts is not a valid argument, but is a demand for total evidence rather than sufficient evidence, something (total evidence) we do not have for any other doctrinal conviction.

    d.   Neither Luther or Calvin clearly held to a view of the errancy of the Bible, but the indication in their writing was a view of inerrancy.

I also listed some lessons I had learned concerning theological debate, perhaps lessons which would emerge in any doctrinal battle, but ones which clearly I had gleaned in this encounter:

1.   Theological debate is necessary for the following reasons:

    the truth must be proclaimed
    the truth must be sharpened
    the truth must be guarded and defended

2.   Theological debate is not easy for the following reasons:

a.   One's own flesh can get in the way

    there must be therefore a concerted effort
        to keep one's heart before the Lord
        to keep a godly attitude in the battle

b.   One's own flesh could lead one to err in one
    of two directions:

    1)   either to overbalance in the direction of
        compromise because of the fear of
        offending someone, or of the desire
        to get along with everyone, or of a
        desire to guard one's career, etc.

    2)   or to err and overbalance on the other side
        of the tension in that one would become
        bitter, and unkind, and unloving, and
        vitriolic in spirit and words to the extent
        that it becomes a personal battle rather
        than a spiritual endeavor to be guided
        by the Holy Spirit of God in action and
        attitude.

c.   One will face the presence of the flesh in others

    which will lead to their evidencing
        a bitter spirit
        an unkind spirit
        an unloving spirit
        a vitriolic spirit

which can evidence itself
in the misunderstanding of one's motives
in the misinterpretation of one's theological
position (the erection of strawmen)
in the mis-application of one's conclusions,

which all are liable to lead
to attacks
to false accusations
upon the opponent's person
upon the opponent's motives
upon the opponent's attitudes,
upon the opponent's character
upon the opponent's personal life

The reality of all of this had become very evident in the heat of the debate we had just been through concerning inerrancy. But there was one more experience which was not only a very difficult application of the above principles, but a very enlightening illustration of them as well.

38

Why Can't We All Just Get Along Together...?

It all came to a head in a time of fellowship over lunch with Dr. Avery at his invitation. After the initial amenities of normal expected conversation, he informed me of his decision, as he began to speak with great sorrow.

"I'm am going to resign as president of the seminary. The pressure is too great over this inerrancy battle! The conservative element is getting stronger, and its just a matter of time now till they will be strong enough to remove me. So I see no reason to wait to be forced out. Its easier to just leave on my own."

"I trust you will understand, sir, when I tell you that I have mixed emotions about that decision!" I admitted.

"Well, I think I know what you mean, but it might be helpful and encouraging to me for you to spell it out for me."

"Sir, I admire you as a man. You are one of the moderates that I greatly admire. You know that I disagree with your theology, and therefore am concerned to move the seminary back to its historic roots, which as you know, I believe to be the verbal inspiration of Scripture. Yet you are a kind and considerate gentleman who has dealt with me in an open and just manner, even giving an avenue of expression for what I think is the truth of Scripture. For that I thank you, and for your character, justice and kindness, I hate to see you go, though I know you must for theological reasons."

"Well, Mr. Pointer, I'm glad I can say the same about you. In this battle, as many on both sides have discredited themselves and their positions, you have evidenced an ability to stand for what you consider the truth and its difficult application (as in your statement that you think it is a necessity for the sake of truth that I leave), yet you have done so with a commendable graciousness in spirit that I have seen in few conservatives. Thank you for the privilege of knowing you and for your help and encouragement just now in my difficult decision."

I saw tears in his eyes, and I replied.

"Sir, I do apologize to you for some of the conservative movement who have not stood for their convictions in a proper manner. Please do not mis-understand these words as a compromise on my part. To me the verbal inspiration of Scripture is an essential doctrine which is the foundation for the understanding and proclamation of all the other doctrines of Scripture. It is essential for a local church's preaching and teaching. It is essential for a Christian college's teaching and training. It is essential for a seminary in the preparation of students for the ministry. Therefore, we cannot compromise this doctrine! We must guard it and keep it and establish it as the basis of all our life and work for Christ. If and when we lose it, we begin a slide towards the weakening of our ministry in every area.

"I will love those who disagree with me in this area, but that love will not let me compromise this essential doctrine which is the basis of the church of the Lord Jesus Christ and its ministry, whatever the cost. It may cost me advancement in career, friends in high or low places, opportunities for pulpits, a misunderstanding of my motives, the smearing of my reputation, or even the loss of my life, but I will not and cannot compromise on this foundational doctrine. I hope you understand my heart and commitment!"

He smiled graciously and replied, "Mr. Pointer, even now in this conversation, you have been an inspiration to me. You have reinforced my conviction that a man must stand for his beliefs, and be willing to suffer for them. Therefore, I gladly will resign as president of this seminary! You do not know it, but I have spoken with Mack Turnover, and he has filled me in, from his research for his article on your past ministry, on what you have suffered thus far in your life for your convictions.[1] Though I disagree with you in many areas, I admire you, and I follow your spirit of conviction in suffering humbly and graciously for one's beliefs as well. I trust we can keep a friendship in the future, and can fellowship from time to time. It has been sweet! Whatever happens to me, don't blame yourself or the conservatives for it. I gladly pay whatever price God asks for the privilege of standing for my convictions. Only pray for me that I may stand with grace and love."

With that we parted, and I never saw him again, because several months after his resignation, he died of an unexpected heart attack. In his passing I lost a friend, and couldn't help but wonder if the battle at the seminary had been a factor in his death.

Of course the moderates used it to shame and blame the conservatives, but I remembered his words: "Whatever happens to me, don't blame yourself or the conservatives for it. I gladly pay whatever price God asks for the privilege of standing for my convictions. Only pray for me that I may stand with grace and love."

I drew some other conclusions from all of this. Though both the conservatives and moderates at times stated those on the other side could not know Christ, I am convinced that there are saved and lost people on both sides. But I am convinced also that there is a tension in the body of Christ between unity and truth. Some press for unity with little concern for the truth. Others press for truth with little concern for unity. Yet there can be no union of even saved people in ministry and service in the body of Christ without an agreement in truth---the essentials of the faith. There cannot be a peace at any price. It would not be possible to have a true unity based on error, nor would it do any good to try to convince ourselves we were in unity, when we were divided over the nature of truth and even its basis. As I had read somewhere, it is better to be divided over the truth than to be united on the basis of error.

Thus I concluded that it would be better for the conservatives and the moderates in the Evangelistic Baptist Convention to go their separate ways, as painful as that might be. Maybe that will come some day, but until it does, the battle will continue because the theological convictions are so diverse.

Yes, the battle which exists now in our convention is and has been a theological one, with the power struggle which exists also being the natural outworking of the theological differences. But the battle is essentially a theological one. The power struggle exists because both sides are strong in their convictions, and convinced they are the possessors of the truth which must lead and govern the denomination for the future. Both are also convinced that the other side and its convictions are a death blow to the convention, either slow or immediate. Thus any hopes of reconciling the two groups in the future, seems to me, to be rather hopeless, unless one side compromises big time, or both sides compromise in smaller ways.

But such compromise is not to be expected, because one would have to face the thorny question of how to synthesize errancy and inerrancy, and their methods of hermeneutics and the doing of theology. The gap between them is not some small creek or ditch, but a giant chasm of major proportions. We are talking about one's authority and basis for knowing the truth. That is gigantic. Is it through an errant Bible or an inerrant Bible? That is major!

And though one can love and respect those with whom he differs, the basis of unity is not there, unless it be on the foundation of either intentional knowledgeable compromise or unintentional ignorant compromise. One who knows the truth, loves the truth, fears the loss of truth and realizes the responsibility of the church to guard the truth, and therefore could have no part in either of the above bases of compromise.

And finally, the battles have just begun! Yes, there are many more battles to come! For with the loss of an inerrant Bible there will come other theological battles. As the inerrantist seeks to stay by the Word of God and be faithful to observe all things the Word commands and teaches, the errantist will be open to the new and latest pragmatic ideas of culture and human reason which contradict the Word of God, whether it be in the area of doctrine or practice.

On that basis I guess I can expect more theological pursuits, and you can expect more "journey" books, the Lord willing, in the days to come!

BOOK LIST
DR. RICHARD P. BELCHER
Richbarry Press, Box 302, Columbia, SC 29202
Phone 803-750-0408 or Fax 798-3190

THEOLOGY

A Comparison of Dispensationalism and Covenant Theology
An objective analysis/comparison of these two systems of theology.

A Layman's Guide to the Lordship Controversy
A summary of the two positions on this important issue---the Lordship and non-lordship views. The author then provides an excellent critique of the non-lordship position based on Scripture.

A Layman's Guide to the Sabbath Question
Co-authored by Richard P. Belcher, Jr., this book presents and compares three current views of the Sabbath---The Seventh Day view, the Christian Sabbath view, and the Lord's Day view.

A Layman's Guide to the Inerrancy Debate
A series of essays answering key questions and objections concerning the doctrine of Biblical inerrancy.

I Believe in Inerrancy
A Biblical, historical and theological presentation of the doctrine of the inspiration of the Scriptures prepared for the layman, but helpful to all.

GREEK HELPS

A Practical Approach to the Greek New Testament
An introduction to a practical use of the Greek NT helpful and useful for both those who have had Greek and those who have not.

Diagramming the Greek New Testament
A self-teaching manual to help one learn to diagram the Greek NT.

Doing an Effective Greek Word Study
A manual which seeks to chart the procedure for doing a Greek word study from the Classical, Hellenistic, New Testament, Patriarchal sources, etc.

Doing Textual Criticism in the Greek New Testament
A manual which seeks to explain in a simple and understandable way the principles and practice of textual criticism in the Greek NT.

Doing Biblical Exegesis
A manual which traces the basic steps in doing Biblical exegesis in a minor or a major manor.

MINISTRY HELPS

All of the following teaching/ministry guides have a clear preachable or teachable outline, which can be easily divided into individual outlines for use in ministry. The introductory material is covered also in the form of an introductory sermon.

1. **Teaching Helps in Psalms**
   A doctrinal study guide which covers the Scriptures, God, man, worship, etc.

2. **Ministry Helps in Isaiah**
   A topical study guide which follows the subjects of the sin of God's people, the judgment of God's people, the solution to the problem of God's people, the future blessings of God's people, etc.

3. **Ministry Helps in Hosea**
   An expositional study guide of Hosea.

4. **Ministry Helps in Amos**
   An expositional study guide of Amos.

5. **Teaching Helps in Malachi**
   An expositional study guide which follows the theme of the burden of Malachi.

6. **Ministry Helps in Luke**
   An expositional study guide of Luke.

7. **Ministry Helps in John**
   An expositional study guide which follows the theme of the Word Christ Jesus as presented, pondered, persecuted, etc.

8. **Ministry Helps in Acts**
   A subject study guide which follows the theme of six provisions God made for world evangelization.

9. **Teaching Helps in I Corinthians**
   An expositional study guide which addresses the many subjects and problems in the church at Corinth---divisions, Christian liberty, the gifts of the Spirit, etc.

10. **Teaching Helps in II Corinthians**
    An expositional study guide which follows the theme of New Testament ministry.

11. **Ministry Helps in Galatians**
    A expositional study guide which follows the theme of Paul's gospel.

12. **Ministry Helps in Ephesians**
    A expositional study guide which follows the theme of the one body of Christ.

13. **Teaching Helps in Hebrews**
    An expositional study guide which follows the theme of the superiority of the New Covenant.

14. **Teaching Helps in James**
    An expositional study guide which follows the theme of practical Christian living.

15. **Teaching Helps in I Peter**
    An expositional study guide which follows the theme of the covenant people of God---their blessings and responsibilities.

Preaching the Gospel-A Theological Perspective & a Personal Method
This work was formerly published as two books. Using I Corinthians 1-4 and II Timothy 3:1-4 as the basis of study, the author sets forth the nature of the gospel we must preach and the nature of the methods we must employ as we preach it. In the second part of the work, the author advances a method of preaching, including the kinds of sermons, the organization of a sermon, the introduction, the body, the main points, the conclusion, the illustrations, the application, and the delivery of the sermon.

THEOLOGICAL NOVELS

A Journey in Grace
This is a theological novel---the story of a young pastor with a typical twentieth century theology, and his pursuit of a burning theological question, which is triggered in his first experience with a pulpit search committee. He cannot and does not rest until he has faced and answered the question, "Young man, are you a Calvinist?"

A Journey in Purity
This is the sequel to the novel *A Journey in Grace*. It is the story of the same pastor in his difficult and heart-braking struggle to bring purity to the corrupt and impure church he pastors. This book identifies with any pastor or church member who has ever wrestled with the principles of church discipline, and their application to a local church.

A Journey in Authority
This is the third in the series of journey books. It is the story of the same young pastor as he wrestles with the question of church government--- congregational-rule versus elder-leadership, along with an attempt to solve a strange mystery threatening the life of one of his members.

A Journey in the Spirit
This continues Pastor Ira Pointer's search for truth---this time in the area of the doctrine of the Holy Spirit. By the meeting of a strange and unique individual, who asks him if he has been filled with the Spirit, he finds himself in the swirl of the modern Pentecostal-Charismatic movement. A shocking surprise ending unmasks the stranger and further opens his eyes to the truth.

A Journey in Inspiration
The story of Ira Pointer's contention for the faith continues as he sets off to seminary, only to find the school deeply committed to a weak view of Scripture. With grace and humility he seeks to stand for the truth of the full inspiration of the Bible, only to find again misunderstanding of his viewpoint and of his motives. His persecution by the "Strawman" assumes major proportion, till God exposes and defeats his opponent in a unique manner.

HISTORICAL STUDIES

Seventeenth Century Baptist Confessions of Faith
Co-authored by Anthony Mattia, this is a discussion and refutation of a modern day claim that the First London Confession in its 1644 and 1646

editions has a different view of the Law than the Second London Confession of 1689.

BOOKS ABOUT A. W. PINK

A. W. Pink---Predestination

An analysis and critique of the central theological theme of A. W. Pink. This work uses the Pink sources to set forth his views of predestination, election and reprobation.

A. W. Pink---Born to Write

This is the second edition of a biography of Pink which first appeared in 1982. The author not only presents the facts of Pink's life, with several chapters of new material possessed by no other biographer, but he also analyzes the life of Pink---his unique personality, his rejection by men, his study methodology, his withdrawal, and his life of isolation during his final years.

Arthur W. Pink---Letters from Spartanburg 1917-1920

A series of about a hundred letters written by Pink when he was pastor of the Northside Baptist Church in Spartanburg, SC 1917-1920. This is the time he wrote his best known book *The Sovereignty of God*. Edited by Dr. Belcher with a complete index for easy use.

Arthur W. Pink---Letters of an Itinerant Preacher 1920-1921

A series of letters written by Pink when he was an itinerant preacher working mostly in the state of California. This was a period when he was wrestling with God's will for his life, whether to continue a public ministry or devote himself exclusively to a writing ministry. Edited by Dr. Belcher with a complete index for easy use.

REPRINTS OF OLDER BOOKS

Luther Rice---Pioneer in Missions and Education

This is an old biography of Luther Rice by Edward B. Pollard and Daniel Gurden Stevens, first published in the first part of the twentieth century. It details the life of Rice and the strong, but sometimes unknown contribution, he made to the cause of modern missions and education in the life of Baptists of America. Prepared for publication by Dr. Belcher